YORK NOTES

Six Women Poets

Notes by James Sale

Longman · York Press

YORK PRESS
322 Old Brompton Road, London SW5 9JH

ADDISON WESLEY LONGMAN LIMITED
Edinburgh Gate, Harlow,
Essex CM20 2JE, United Kingdom
Associated companies, branches and representatives throughout the world

© Librairie du Liban *Publishers* 1998

First published 1998

ISBN 0–582–36840–5

Designed by Vicki Pacey, Trojan Horse, London
Illustrated by Sarah Young
Phototypeset by Gem Graphics, Trenance, Mawgan Porth, Cornwall
Colour reproduction and film output by Spectrum Colour
Produced by Addison Wesley Longman China Limited, Hong Kong

CONTENTS

PREFACE

York Notes are designed to give you a broader perspective on works of literature studied at GCSE and equivalent levels. We have carried out extensive research into the needs of the modern literature student prior to publishing this new edition. Our research showed that no existing series fully met students' requirements. Rather than present a single authoritative approach, we have provided alternative viewpoints, empowering students to reach their own interpretations of the text. York Notes provide a close examination of the work and include biographical and historical background, summaries, glossaries, analyses of characters, themes, structure and language, cultural connections and literary terms.

If you look at the Contents page you will see the structure for the series. However, there's no need to read from the beginning to the end as you would with a novel, play, poem or short story. Use the Notes in the way that suits you. Our aim is to help you with your understanding of the work, not to dictate how you should learn.

York Notes are written by English teachers and examiners, with an expert knowledge of the subject. They show you how to succeed in coursework and examination assignments, guiding you through the text and offering practical advice. Questions and comments will extend, test and reinforce your knowledge. Attractive colour design and illustrations improve clarity and understanding, making these Notes easy to use and handy for quick reference.

York Notes are ideal for:
- Essay writing
- Exam preparation
- Class discussion

The author of these Notes is James Sale. James is an experienced teacher and has worked extensively with students on various examinations. He has been a Head of Drama and a Head of English as well as Deputy Headmaster in two schools. He is an author of over twenty books.

The text used in these Notes is from the Oxford Student Texts Edition, edited by Judith Kinsman, 1992.

Health Warning: **This study guide will enhance your understanding, but should not replace the reading of the original text and/or study in class.**

INTRODUCTION

HOW TO STUDY A POEM

You have bought this book because you wanted to study poetry on your own. This may supplement work done in class.

- Look at the poem. How are the lines organised? Are they in groups? Are any lines repeated? Are any of the lines shorter or longer than the others? Try to think of reasons why the poet set out the lines in this way.
- Do lots of the lines end with a comma or a full stop – or does the sense carry over on to another line? What is the effect of stopping at the end of each line?
- Read the poem out aloud (or aloud in your head). Does the poem rhyme? If so, what words rhyme? Is this important ? Do some lines almost rhyme? Do some lines have rhyming words inside the line? If there is no rhyme, think about why the poet stops each line where he/she does.
- Read the poem aloud again. Think about the rhythm. Listen for the stressed words. Does the pattern of stressed and unstressed syllables create any kind of mood? Does it match the mood or subject-matter of the poem? Have some words been chosen for their sound?
- What is the poem about? Do not make up your mind too soon. Your first thoughts need to be reassessed when you reach the end. Remember that the subject-matter and the theme or idea of the poem may not be the same.
- Do any words make you stop and think? Are there interesting or unusual combinations of words? (Check the meaning of any words which puzzle you – they may have a meaning you are not familiar with.)

The Six Women Poets contained in this selection are all contemporary poets who continue to write. Poets who are worth reading continue to speak to fresh readers in succeeding generations. The advantage of reading contemporary poets is that their work has a particular relevance, since it arises from the culture and concerns which directly affect us. Of course, the disadvantage is that it is difficult to be entirely 'objective' about our contemporaries – we may feel strongly partisan about the issues of our day in a way in which we cannot feel about issues in, say, John Milton's or Emily Dickinson's day. Furthermore, being contemporary – living – poets means their work is not complete: there is more to come. Any judgements we make, then, on their work must of necessity be tentative and provisional. As Dr Johnson observed in the context of Shakespeare's enduring reputation: 'What mankind have long possessed they have often examined and compared, and if they persist to value the possession, it is because frequent comparisons have confirmed opinion in its favour'.

There are two major issues to consider in looking at the historical and social context of Six Women Poets. The first is that the anthology groups women together at all. Our age is one in which the voice of women demands to be heard in every forum. Labels – such as 'feminist' – are not generally helpful whenever usage has obscured precise meanings. Doubtless not all of the six poets would want to be called feminists. There is a world of difference between the voices of Selima Hill and that of Liz Lochhead, between Carol Rumens and Gillian Clarke, and between Grace Nichols and Fleur Adcock. But they do have one thing in common: their own voice is unmistakably female, and at the same time each generalises about the female role. And of all the roles that women adopt the one we find common – and

What beliefs and values do you attach to the word 'mother'? Have your ideas changed as you have grown older?

central – to all six writers in this selection is that of the mother. To study 'mother' in these six poets is to study how roles and perceptions and values have changed in post-war society.

Second, the influence of the twentieth century movement known as Modernism is everywhere evident in the work of the Six Women Poets. A look at the Form Sheet (p. 9) will leave one in little doubt that the breakdown of traditional forms of poetry leaves **free verse** (see Literary Terms) the most dominant (anti-?) form. A possibly even more revealing sign is that none of the poets usually commences their first lines (except when starting a sentence) with a capital letter – a traditional poetic requirement. However, notice how, for example, Carol Rumens reverts to the tradition when using **blank verse** or a **ballad metre** (see Literary Terms), namely, a traditional form. The old certainties and their requirements and prescriptive models have largely passed away, and in their place is a new searching – an exploratory mode – which is often akin to ruminating aloud. We follow each thrust and turn of their thinking and feeling as they range over their ideas and experiences.

There is in this, then, a paradox: Modernism was a symptom of the breakdown of shared values in society at large. In poetic terms this manifested itself in avoidance of well-known **metres** (see Literary Terms) and forms, and an emphasis on individuality which created its own rhythms and shapes without reference, except sometimes **allusively** (see Literary Terms) and obliquely, to the past. However, the linking of the Six Women Poets and the stereotyping of them as 'feminists' tends to indicate a set of shared values. Thus it is important to stress that while it is true that they do speak of and for women, and also for the wider community in places, at heart – as with all true poets –

they speak for themselves individually, and the language they forge is their own. To summarise: we should look for differences as much as we look for common themes and ideas in their work.

FORM SHEET

The Form Sheet (p. 9) is a handy way of seeing the preferred forms of writing of each of the poets It is also a useful way of cross-referencing their work.

If we take the first point, then we see that Gillian Clarke, Grace Nichols, Carol Rumens and Liz Lochhead are much more drawn to **free verse** (see Literary Terms) forms than Fleur Adcock and Selima Hill. We might want to ask why this is. How does form match the subject matter they each are writing about? We notice, too, in looking at the chart, that rhyme is the exception rather than the rule – what does this relate to? Possibly, a world in which euphony (or, pleasing sound, which is what rhyme creates) is inappropriate?

If we take the second point, then this Form Sheet should enable us to make interesting connections and comparisons: both Gillian Clarke and Carol Rumens write **ballads** (see Literary Terms), so it might be useful to compare them. Equally, why did Carol Rumens choose to use **blank verse** (see Literary Terms) for one of her poems when she is quite happy using free verse for many others? Was it because the historical subject matter demanded a certain 'elevation' of style?

Here is not the place to give answers to these questions, but to suggest ways in which the Form Sheet can be used as a constructive way of looking at each poet's work, as well as enabling the reader to see connections between the poets.

the form	CLARKE	NICHOLS	ADCOCK	RUMENS	HILL	LOCHHEAD
free verse	letter from a far country** marged siege last rites still life	waterpot like a flame we the women i coming back 'Realities' of black women in my name up my spine be a butterfly iguana memory waiting for thelma's laughter	last song*	at puberty one street beyond two women days and nights december walk unplayed music tides	chicken feathers the flowers	the offering the teachers the prize revelation an abortion poppies a giveaway** the other woman storyteller the father the mother spinster** everybody's mother fat girl's confession**
three line stanzas		those women* praise song for my mother*	earlswood*	the advanced set carpet-weavers, morocco		
four line stanzas/ quatrains	white roses		nature table street song** witnesses	a marriage		laundrette**
stanzaic (no. lines per stanza)	miracle on st david's day* (5) east moons (5) login (5) scything (7) the sundial(12)		loving hitler (5) for heidi with blue hair (5) outwood (6) the keepsake* (6) tadpole (7) the telephone call (8)	gifts and loans (5) dream of south africa (6)	dewpond & black drainpipes (5) among the thyme & daisies (5) down by the sally gardens(7) the fowlers of the marsh (8) below hekla (9) the goose (13) diving at midnight (13) the bicycle ride (14)	
couplets			the chiffonier the prize winning poem	over the bridge		
sestinas				rules for beginners		
ballad	overheard in county sligo			ballad of the morning after		
blank verse				the girl in the cathedral		
shape		sugar cane				

* indicates a regular stanzaic structure, but which includes some variation(s)

** indicates some usage of rhyme in the poem

TWO

SUMMARIES

GILLIAN CLARKE

BACKGROUND

Gillian Clarke was born in 1937 in Cardiff and has been a part-time lecturer and also an editor. She is very much a poet of place – in her case, Wales – and sees her own responsibilities as being those of a poet who is the 'voice of the tribe'. All her poems are true stories and so language is the means by which experience can be shared. It has, therefore, a communal function. Critics have commented that poems like her *Letter from a Far Country* move as if a whole community were behind it. Moreover, her work discovers links between the past and present, the human and the natural world, the animate and inanimate. It seeks to explore, basically, those things which endure. In that sense Gillian Clarke's poetry is not about ephemera, or the fashionable.

LETTER FROM A FAR COUNTRY

All the songs of tradition only allow males to depart.

The poet writes a letter from an imaginary place, perhaps in the future, to men who are husbands, fathers and ancestors. The waste and order of family life are presented. The order is sweet and will persist even when she is gone. Although far away, the poet sees her environment as being a hilly, feminine landscape. Typically, her grandmother might have been there. Men control the gates to it, and prevent women leaving. From this vantage point the poet sees the men's activities as being a form of wild opposition, which becomes a chaotic series of bewildering incidents. Much of it emerges from a frightening darkness. Dark rivers penetrate the hills – the female environment – and in them children are lost. Eventually, however, a music is formed through the natural processes as personified by the 'Piper'. The poet tells us to listen to the life forces that overcome the death forces of winter.

Focusing on her grandmother, the poet shows a woman who carries on despite the great destruction of wars. The landscape of women is contrasted with the seascape of men. What her grandmother did is described in loving detail; it contrasts with the sexual restlessness of men as they engage with women. A series of six parenthetical comments appear; these are asides and **homilies** (see Literary Terms). The first tells us women, through their planning, cater for all 'your needs'.

Complex **images** (see Literary Terms) of sheets, sea, herring gulls and men convey several ideas. That women control men through repeated sexual experience; but that men are wild and cold and do not have the warmer satisfactions of women. Men break free of women and mock them, but this is because they are envious. Men, like the gulls, always seem to cast shadows. In the face of this women lose their spontaneity and seek to preserve what is natural by bottling it. This process preserves important memories. Thus women's work becomes religious in its significance.

Men, meanwhile, are planting barley. The poet recalls her own girlhood desire to be out helping them. But this desire leads to pain, either of the menstrual flow or the loss of virginity. As she reflects on this, she leaps ahead to give a best recipe for bread. Then she goes back to the history of the parish – its vitality and its inhabitants are described, including its paupers.

In the present, the poet finds that the industrial stream is cleaner than it once was. Nevertheless, the sea still washes up its dead-markings. It cannot in fact hope to clean itself, although it constantly tries. We are invited to investigate our own contribution to all the filth.

The innocent suffer. Suicide afflicts the woman who was poor, isolated and despairing, although a birth in the room where she died helps mitigate the fact. More mysteriously, a woman who had everything, inexplicably, killed herself. The landscape collects all the talk and conversation and converts it into a natural music.

Women prefer a much more natural type of religion, earth-rooted, but one which has compassion at its heart.

This natural music contrasts with that of the enemy, probably organised religion, which helps men enslave women. Love should be loose, not a tight collar. What is a woman's role? The poet reflects on how she responds to the current of men. Ultimately, women will fulfil their obligations, but they will give back to women what has been appropriated by men. Two **stanzas** (see Literary Terms) contrast the voices of dead grandmothers and their call to their daughters to stay at home and do their necessary work, and the graves of dead grandfathers which only promote their own virtue but without anything meaningful to say.

The poet concludes that women are trained to be mothers: they can hear the needs of their children. This commitment means they will not leave home. In fact, the poem is interrupted by the need to collect children from school. The poem is unfinished. Three short rhyming **quatrains** (see Literary Terms) celebrate women's vital role. But the celebration is also a challenge: if women fail to do their work, who else could do it?

COMMENT   The poem is a **free verse** (see Literary Terms) meditation on the role of women in society and an answer to the question posed to women by men in the poem: 'Where are your great works?'. Women do great things but not necessarily in ways that men define as great. This poem seeks to redefine what it means to do great things by focusing on what women actually achieve.

The poem works by a series of contrasts. Essentially, the landscape is feminine and this is contrasted with the

The central question for every body is: what values are important in life?

seascape, which is masculine. This exploration leads to a sense of the rooted, homeliness of the women and their sense of order and purpose. Men represent a dangerous strength which is invariably misused.

The form of the poem is **epistolary** (see Literary Terms), but this is not a real letter for two reasons: first, it is unfinished and unsent. Ironically, and naturally, what women do stops them completing these other works that men value. Secondly, the title of the poem, *Letter from a Far Country*, indicates that the address from which the poem is sent is imaginary.

MIRACLE ON ST DAVID'S DAY

A beautiful afternoon is described in what appears to be a spacious country house. The second stanza (see Literary Terms) abruptly explains that the poet is reading poetry to inmates of a mental asylum. Three inmates are described. As the poet observes them, a fourth is led to sit down and listen to her speaking.

This man has been dumb for some forty years. Listening, he gently sways to the rhythm of her poetry. Suddenly he stands up. The poet feels afraid. Then, the man recites William Wordsworth's poem *The Daffodils*. The effect is instantaneous: this is not what is supposed to happen. The poet contrasts the man with the daffodils outside: they, too, are still and the colours of their beauty remain unspoken.

It was forty years before that the man learnt *The Daffodils* poem by rote. Since then he has been dumb and miserable, though always aware that there was a music in speech. After he has finished his recitation, the group collectively notice the flowers' silence. A solitary bird sings nearby; the daffodils appear with the intensity of a flame.

COMMENT

The fact that a man who has been dumb for forty years or so and now speaks is itself remarkable enough, but the title adds more. First, it places it within the context of St David – a Christian and Welsh patron saint. St David's Day points to the essential Welshness of the occasion, coinciding with the onset of spring, renewal and victory.

LOGIN

The opening **stanza** (see Literary Terms) depicts the scene: chapel and bridge. The bridge, significantly, connects across the river. It enables the poet and her son to visit an old neighbour, and to return. After they have talked, the old woman 'ruffles' the son's hair with her old hand. This affectionate gesture reveals that the old woman had once loved the poet's father. Presumably, she is now 'seeing' him in the grandson.

Images (see Literary Terms) of water suggest how quickly time has separated her from their life. Exchanged glances cannot 'span' such turbulence. Whatever happened between this old woman and the poet's father is now beyond recapture.

In 'Miracle on St David's Day' it is the big, dumb man who through poetry breaks the silence; in 'Login' it is the old woman's touch which stretches across the years through the poet's art.

Despite the power of the river, the thrush outsings it – the poet's own art can make a bridge between the love that existed then and what is now. (This contrasts with the village at lunch – people going about their ordinary business, not thinking about these sorts of things.) The river divided the cow parsley, but now the cow parsley covers the bridge, and a link is made. Time's river washes away life and love, but poetry testifies to love's enduring quality. The final stanza contrasts the light on the bridge with the shadow where she is. Even the 'linking' moment now will become a past moment. And she, too, will become part of that division created by fast water. Even the future will fade.

THE SUNDIAL

The poet's son is ill and having nightmares about lions. When he gets up the son decides to create a sundial from a paper circle he places on the grass. All day the son speaks about time, and all day he and the poet feel and watch the movement of the sun. The fact that the sun has to move along its path suggests that it is caged. This word recalls the lions of the nightmares – the sun may be caged, and so less dangerous, but its pointing with a black stick indicates eventual death. The hand of the clock points to time, but this really means it points to each individual, and this is something adults experience.

COMMENT

The structure of the poem is ingenious: two **stanzas** (see Literary Terms) of 12 lines each constitute a total of 24 lines, which mirrors the 24 hours of the day. Furthermore, the contrast between night and day, adult and child, lions and sun, all suggest a two-fold pattern, which the poem imitates.

SCYTHING

Spring is well under way and the garden needs to be tidied up. The poet inadvertently slashes a nesting willow warbler's eggs: the mess on the blade is described and the **compound word** (see Literary Terms) 'baby-bones' is **emotive** (see Literary Terms). The poet and her son are both disturbed by this, and blame each other. In silence the willow warbler repeats her question. Presumably, 'Why?'. The poet returns to the scene with the pieces of the accident. Initially, these pieces are warm on the knife — and that reminds the poet of how warm birth fluids are. This reminder recalls her own son's birth — she identifies with the willow warbler's loss.

COMMENT   The poem simply describes the scene. There is a deep respect for the bird — it has, after all, a crown which she has made it lose. Dylan's pain is different from his mother's, as the word 'separate' indicates. He is upset because the innocent chicks in the eggs have been destroyed. His mother's concerns are also with the hurt inflicted on an innocent and beautiful bird.

MARGED

The poet thinks of the previous occupant of the house, Marged. The poet has created an extra room above where Marged lived and died, alone and penniless. The poet's situation is very different: the gold of her whisky suggests opulence. When the poet parks her car she can see the track that Marged used. And she can see, too, the hills that Marged must have seen. Digging in her garden she unearths the 'broken crocks' Marged must have used. What else did they have in common? Both are women.

COMMENT   The poem describes the shared experiences of living in the same house as a previous occupant. Her experiences, though, are fundamentally different from Marged's grinding poverty. The sentences describing the poet's life in the centre of the poem lack main verbs – they are static and do not connect with Marged's life.

SIEGE

Even as a baby in   The poet sits in her kitchen sorting family photographs.
her father's arms   Her background radio describes some faraway catastro-
she wants to move   phe. She sees a photograph of herself when a baby in
away from his   her father's arms. The poet describes her garden's
control.   profusion of colours and plants. Flowers are depicted in terms of clothing and dress. From the darkness daisies are bursting out. Now she studies a photograph of her mother in her summer dress. She remembers another field beyond the photograph – a field of fear.

The afternoon is wearing on. The focus in the garden switches from plants to insects and then to birds. A yellow butterfly starts flying over the lawn. In the kitchen radio voices suddenly become urgent: the peace is shattered. A woman is screaming. Incidents on the radio appear to be happening in the garden and the kitchen: floors collapse and machine guns are firing. The song of the wren is no longer 'sweet': it is a song of growing lust. On the lawn 'figures' are crystal clear – as is the yellow butterfly, almost at its destination. The nameless 'figures', too, are almost ready to pounce.

COMMENT   The poem weaves together three strands: the beauty of the poet's garden, the **images** (see Literary Terms) of

her photographs from the past, and the actual siege
of the Iranian embassy during the 1980s. A series
of contrasts connects these things: the photographs
show people and family, but also connects them to
the plants, animals and fields. Although beautiful,
there is something dangerous in them: the daisies
and their 'deep / original root'. From a distance the
wren is sweet, but the real meaning of its song is
lustful and rapacious. Cleverly, the poet does not
identify which 'birds' are the 'figures' on the lawn,
despite their being so clear. Like storming SAS troops,
their outline may be clear, but their faces are all
hidden.

OVERHEARD IN COUNTY SLIGO

Five **quatrains** (see Literary Terms) in a roughly **ballad
metre** (see Literary Terms) recount the life and feelings
of a woman from County Roscommon. The italics

Note the contrast
between 'in the lap
of the land' and
the phrase 'back of
beyond'.

indicate actual words spoken. The situation on the farm
is described, and then the road of escape is noted. She
wanted to be an actress or a writer. Instead, she's
cleaning the house and looking at her own face in the
mirror. She should feel happy, but it doesn't feel as if
she is.

EAST MOORS

A bitter April is coming to an end; cherries are
flowering. In the distance the steelworks no longer
smoke. The poet in the past was so accustomed to the
sights and smells of the steelworks that they seemed
almost natural. One consequence of the closure will be
that washing hung out to dry will remain clean.
Another consequence will be the wives of various men
organising jobs for them to do, since the men are now
unemployed.

A few men stayed on till the bitter end – saw all the things that gave their life meaning demolished. This reminds the poet of the time her own children were taken to see two water cooling towers blown up.

Fate seems blind to the sufferings of the people. Somehow their absence created a tremendous void. May has come – and the bitterness is now icy. The town will be cleaner without the steelworks, but it will be poorer too. The cherries flower. But the sky is bitter white.

The poem explores what happens when a community – the East Moors of the title – loses it major employer, the steelworks. We come to the end of April, which itself had been bitter, expecting to find summer. Instead the weather is even worse, as is the situation for the people.

LAST RITES

The road retains its markings of dust and barley seed. These are 'stigmata' – wounds of Christ. The second **stanza** (see Literary Terms) moves on to describe the inquest story of a road accident. There the poet feels the cyclist's dead pulse and covers him with her own grey blanket. As she does so, she also tenderly touches his face. Moving away, his blood is on her hands and his darling ('cariad'), the pillion passenger, is being supported in her arms. Driving the passenger home from the inquest, they share a vision of everything subjected to breakage and cruelty.

COMMENT

The tone of the poem elegiac. The title is important. Initially, the poet is on her way to Synod Inn. Synod suggests a religious meeting, although the Inn is a place of refreshment and pleasure. But the word 'stigmata' again reinforces our sense of the spiritual. In fact, the poet acts as a substitute priest for the dead young man – in that sense supplying 'last rites'.

STILL LIFE

The poet reflects that polishing brass ornaments with a friend was a good thing to do. Polishing the brass was like polishing their friendship – making it cleaner and brighter, revealing new patterns. However, the poet appeared sad, and this puzzled the friend. The poet had discovered that each object remained cold, unless it were reflecting another's warmth.

WHITE ROSES

Outside a green room, white roses bloom. Inside a boy is dying. Death is like a 'bloom' spreading in his body. He is sleeping, but wakes as the poet enters. He is in dreadful pain, which he quietly endures. There is some reprieve – sometimes he feels better. When that happens he talks again and plays with his cat. Meanwhile, the sun goes about its business, and the cat hunts birds. Unconcerned, the rose outside the room will survive longer than the child.

'diamond paws' contrast with the boy's unsubstantial flesh.

COMMENT

The central contrast is the between the boy dying in agony, and nature's indifference. The use of colours is evocative: the green room itself suggests a place of natural processes; as 'white' is a sepulchral colour. The association of the roses with death is further enhanced with the comparison with [bone] 'white china'. Red, meanwhile, suggests blood and pain.

THEMES, LANGUAGE & STYLE

Gillian Clarke's poetry concerns a number of significant themes and images (see Literary Terms). Thematically, her poems explore family life, the role of women and the role of outsiders generally. These are not dealt with exclusively in poems, often the themes are interwoven.

A poem, for example, such as 'Marged' clearly has a dual focus on the role of women and the fact that Marged herself was such an outsider. Her most ambitious poem, *Letter from a Far Country*, covers all three themes in great detail.

Her most significant imagery (see Literary Terms) involves colour, sound and natural life: seasons, climate, animals and plants. The use of the colour yellow/gold in so many poems suggests it has a particular significance for her. Compare the use of yellow in 'Siege' with its use in 'Still Life'. Equally, and as befits a poet, sound is crucial in her work – and the frequent allusions to its absence. In 'Login' it is the moment 'without words' where all the significance resides. The seasons, climates, and their crops of plants and animals all richly feature. Sometimes she creates what is called the pathetic fallacy (see Literary Terms) – nature reflects human feelings. For example, the 'bitter April' of 'East Moors' reflects the bitter feelings of the community. But at other times nature is sublimely indifferent to human feelings and purposes. This is most obviously demonstrated in 'White Roses' – the sun, the cat and the rose carry on regardless of the boy's suffering and eventual death.

Finally, she is very much a poet of place, and her place is within the Welsh community. Her diction frequently reflects this. There are topographical references, as well as words of distinct Welsh origin. This is important, particularly in a poem such as *Letter from a Far Country*. The use of actual Welsh words for grandmother and grandfather establishes a much more intimate link with them. It is for her, as the concluding lines of the poem assert, a mother tongue. By saying this, of course, we come full circle: the language itself being a *mother* tongue that says something about her key thematic preoccupation with the role of women in the world.

TEST YOURSELF (Gillian Clarke)

 Identify the poems from which these words are taken.

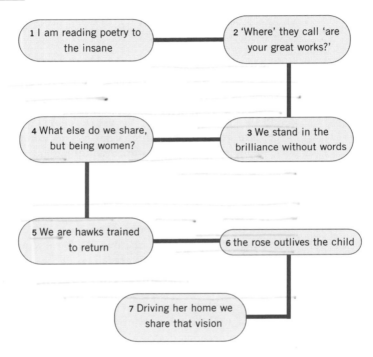

1 I am reading poetry to the insane

2 'Where' they call 'are your great works?'

4 What else do we share, but being women?

3 We stand in the brilliance without words

5 We are hawks trained to return

6 the rose outlives the child

7 Driving her home we share that vision

Check your answers on page 96.

 Consider these issues.

a How Gillian Clarke explores family life.

b What Gillian Clarke's view of the role of women is.

c The contrast between life and death in Gillian Clarke's poetry.

d The use of natural imagery in her work.

e How colours highlight key ideas in her poetry.

GRACE NICHOLS

BACKGROUND

Grace Nichols was in born 1950 in Guyana and has been a reporter and journalist. She emigrated to Britain in 1977. Apart from writing poetry, she is also a novelist. She writes as a Caribbean poet trying to reclaim the language heritage of her ancestors. The reclamation of the language is also a political statement – it is a rejection of slavery and the inheritance of inferiority. At the same time, Grace Nichols is careful to reject any suggestion of stereotyping that resisting oppression may give rise to. Her language critically examines the 'woolly' concepts that sometimes accompany protestations and '-isms' of race or gender. There is a marked social conscience in her work, and an eye for the details which comprise ordinary living.

WATERPOT

The daily routine of slaves going to work in the sugar cane fields is depicted. They are treated very badly, like animals. However, one woman attempts to retain her dignity by holding herself erect – held high, as it were. There is a royalty of movement about her. The overseer tries to make them move faster and sneers at the pathetic attempt of the woman to hold herself high. But, the poet comments, the woman's dignity and poise are absolutely natural to her.

COMMENT Notice the repetition of language – 'darkness', 'quickening', 'pathetic' – which indicates the strength of feelings involved, and also creates a sense of 'rush' appropriate to what the overseer is attempting to do – hurry them on and undermine the confidence of the woman. The 'O' is a deep felt exclamation, which reverses the overseer's opinions.

SUGAR CANE

The poem explores the paradox of the sugar cane: hard on the outside, but soft inside – his movements are a cry for help. His colour is an illness and just before a storm sugar cane suffers a sort of fever. He has no control of how he grows – we help him do that. But as he gets bigger, helped by sun and rain, we kill him. He can't survive. Growth is painful for sugar cane – as he grows he learns how many crimes his existence has come to claim. Sugar cane casts a shadow on the earth, and is alone apart from his mistress, the wind. This mistress – despite his 'hardness' – gets close and intimate with him. The poet quietly positions herself beneath the two of them – perhaps enacting the slave's role in the growth of the cane.

The poet's fascination with the process is almost voyeuristic.

'Sugar Cane' explores the parallels between the actual sugar cane and the lives of the slaves who produced it. Both give their lives – their juice inside – to produce the sweetness for others. The basic technique is one of **personification** (see Literary Terms): sugar cane and the wind become 'people' with emotions and feelings – his 'hard reserve' and she 'caressing'. Notice that the poem is laid out in five irregular **stanzas** (see Literary Terms) that contain very short lines: these 'reflect' the sugar cane stalks – in the fourth stanza it is particularly high.

LIKE A FLAME

This poem charts the natural attraction between a man and woman. Nothing has been said, but she laughs, and is attracted to him. He's soft and quick, even spiritual. She acknowledges him, decides she likes him, and determines to meet him that night. She is 'hot' for him.

COMMENT

'my eyes / make four / with this man' shows how important the 'look' is in mutual attraction. The 'prayer' image (see Literary Terms) suggests love's religious significance. Finally, the 'flame' not only suggests her heat, but also her radiance – love ignites the personality.

WE THE WOMEN

The poet identifies with all the women who are effectively working hard as slaves. They create an environment which simply gives them pain – and they die ignored and forgotten.

COMMENT

There is a great deal of empathy with the suffering of others in Grace Nichols's poetry.

The resilience and strength of the women is contrasted with their appalling treatment. Notice the compound words (see Literary Terms)– 'ache-and-pain-a-me' and 'back-o-hardness' – which create, in the way the words roll off the tongue, a casual sense of describing and enduring suffering. The first person plural – 'we' – reinforces the poet's solidarity with those who've suffered.

I COMING BACK

This poem is one of retribution and haunting. The 'I' of the poem is coming back to haunt the 'Massa', or master who had mistreated the slaves.

COMMENT The use of repetition here is very effective in conveying the sense of menace against the 'Massa'.

GLOSSARY Massa master

UP MY SPINE

The poet sees an old, crippled woman. She describes her dreadful infirmities in great detail. Yet, when she looks in her eye the woman laughs – a laugh so chilling that the poet is shocked.

COMMENT

The sights are external; but the laughter comes from a 'bone' within.

This is a simple but effective poem. Each **stanza** (see Literary Terms) except the last is introduced by 'I see'. The vivid description is gripping and graphic, but does not intimidate the poet in any way. But switching from seeing to hearing does – the sound of her laugh frightens the poet.

OF COURSE WHEN THEY ASK FOR POEMS ABOUT THE 'REALITIES' OF BLACK WOMEN

The poem is an answer to those who want stereotypes of what black women are like. These people want a 'bleeding-heart' effect – suffering and downtrodden. They can only see black women as a stereotype they already possess. Sometimes, though, they want a 'perfect song' – perhaps as if singing about their condition would make it right. However, the poet feels no poem she could write would be big enough to describe any kind of woman, not just a black one. There are such contrasts in black women.

The poet concludes that what she wants to see is black women out there in the world, fully confident, and treading down all the negative history that they've endured and inherited. In such a situation the walk of the women would be a 'dancing step'.

COMMENT

The tone of this poem is joyful – asserting the strength and variety of black women – whilst at the same time being somewhat exasperated. Clearly, some sense of pique induced her to write the poem because she was fed up with being asked to write it. Probably, the stereotyping underpinning such a request was a primary cause of irritation. Notice that while the poet is keen to celebrate black women, and does so, she does not exclude other women from praise. Her language is direct and **colloquial**. The **compound words** (see Literary Terms) like 'full-of-we-selves' effectively convey the sense of fullness of personality.

GLOSSARY   **piece-a-pussy** vagina, the slang expression suggests prostituting
                  the body to feed the children
                  that see than see
                  pickney children
                  dem they

IN MY NAME

The **persona** (see Literary Terms) of the poem is a
woman having a child. She describes her belly and
commands the earth to receive the child. She then
provides a blessing that gives her 'perfect' child a series
of names which are reflections on his origin from mixed
blood. A final adjuration insists that no harm or evil

The poem is a   comes near her child. This child may be the product of
kind of prayer for   mixed blood, but her own blood, and the tears she spilt,
the child's safety.   cleanse and provide an environment for the child to
swim in.

COMMENT   The poem shows the warm affection the mother bears
towards her child, despite the fact that it is born out of
wedlock ('bastard fruit') and is the result of sex between
her black self and a white man. Society may disapprove,
because the child is 'tainted'; but for her the child is
'perfect'. The title echoes and transforms the phrase 'In
the Name of the Father'.

ALA

A black woman is being executed. She is eaten alive by
ants. Her crime was killing her new-born child to
prevent it becoming just another slave – dead, the child
is 'free'. The woman is to be made an example of.
While this is going on, the women cry and sing as they
go about their work. The poet cries out to the goddess,
Ala. She tells her that she is soon to be joined by Uzo,
the woman to be killed, and asks that at least her
remains are laid to rest. She also requests – this time

recognising Ala as a Mother herself – that Uzo be permitted to enter the 'pocket of your womb', so that she can rest. A parallel is drawn between the womb of birth – life – and the womb of death.

COMMENT

'O' is a form of solemn address and suitable for a supplicant asking her diety for help

This poem vividly contrasts with 'In my Name' where the child is tenderly loved. Uzo has rejected her child and is being condemned for its murder. However, the situation is not clear cut – the reasons for killing her child do evoke the sympathy of the poet, as does the terrible cruelty of the death ordained her.

CARIBBEAN WOMAN PRAYER

This poem is in Creole. A woman tells God to wake up, start looking, and see her prayer on behalf of an oppressed people. God is a Mother, Father, Sister, Brother, and a Holy Fire. She hardly needs to tell God how things are, because God knows. The devil walks the land: the children are hungry and forks don't tuck into food, but stones. It might be raining but there's really a drought, and the men are desperately trying to calculate what they can do.

God knows the people are proud and generous, and also ashamed. They are reduced to feeding like chicken in a yard. Politics and trickery are responsible for this. She asks God to give politicians courage and true insight, so that things can grow. That way the people, too, won't walk in doubt. People are at the heart of a community – they're not just some adjunct to the United States of America – there to be shot down by vested interests.

What she wants is to see the children waking up happy, with enough food to eat. To see them exercising healthy limbs and going to sleep on a full stomach. She wants to see the current hopelessness replaced with real life and a sense of winning achievement.

And she wants to see men and women fully possessing their lives.

She ends by shouting out praise to God.

COMMENT   The title includes the word 'prayer' and so the liturgical language is not surprising. Clearly, the community is in a state of extremity – hence the boldness with which she approaches God, and at the same time the humility as she acknowledges God's knowledge of events. Poverty, ignorance, despair and corruption are all themes which surface in her exploration of the Caribbean world. God is invariably referred to as a 'He' in Christian terms. In this poem the Trinity of God the Father, Son and Holy Spirit has given way to a five-personed God where Mudder and Sister precede Fadder and Brudder.

GLOSSARY   **de** the
dis this
tings things
kyant can't
mek make
Rodney and Bishop two leading citizens allegedly assassinated by outside influence
hibiscus rose mallow plant (noted for its reds and whites)

BE A BUTTERFLY

The sinner is like a caterpillar in that it is trapped on a 'fleshy' leaf; the saint is like Jesus and the butterfly in that they soar towards heaven.

A sermon from an old preacher tells the poet to imitate the higher life of Jesus by being a butterfly, and not a caterpillar. The second **stanza** (see Literary Terms) describes the preacher working up a sweat as he gets into his sermon, no matter that the church is half-empty. His audience can barely contain their laughter – only the father of the poet's family keeps a straight face. Afterwards they go home and enjoy a Sunday meal. The poet repeats the essential message of the preacher –

be a butterfly – and agrees that this is the best way to be.

C<small>OMMENT</small> The preacher is illustrating his religious point – probably that believing in Jesus means being reborn – by using the **metaphor** (see Literary Terms) of the caterpillar's conversion into a butterfly. The preacher means well – and there is probably admiration for his performance, given the 'half-empty' church. But he is too serious for his own good. Father, too, it seems.

T<small>HOSE</small> <small>WOMEN</small>

The poet sees women, cut and working really hard, attempting to land fresh shrimps in their nets. They are standing up to their waists in water, which seems to cling sensually to them. The poet remembers them 'fishing' as it were, when she was a child – they caught her attention. And the poet saw 'fish' slipping through their laughing thighs.

C<small>OMMENT</small> This is a sensually charged poem. The poet remembers these women, and admires them. She remembers them as a child – they had a confidence about them. 'Voluptuousness' suggests full physical beauty and with a large dose of sexual appeal. The final **image** (see Literary Terms) of 'fish' and 'eels' can be variously interpreted: it is literally true, but also it is suggestive of fecundity, of male semen, and of life itself. These women are vitally alive, and draw life to themselves.

P<small>RAISE</small> <small>SONGS</small> <small>FOR</small> <small>MY</small> <small>MOTHER</small>

'you said' – past tense – helps us feel the sense of loss.

Her mother is depicted is a series of four short **stanzas** (see Literary Terms). She was deep, brave and penetrating; she was attractive, various and protective; she was an inspiration, a warmth and a source of

energy; she was the ultimate source of sustenance. The
fifth and final stanza shows the mother issuing an order
to the poet to go out to 'wide futures'.

COMMENT   The form of the poem is interesting: the repetition of
'You were' followed by lines which do not involve a past
tense verb – 'deep and bold and fathoming', for
example, creates a vivid sense of the mother's qualities
still being present – 'replenishing replenishing' being
the satisfying final example.

IGUANA MEMORY

The poet recounts an incident of encountering a iguana
in her backyard. The poem describes the hurried
movements of the lizard, and her sense of its large size.
It stopped briefly, and each looked at the other. Then,
it rushed off 'for the green of its life'.

COMMENT   The language in this poem is particularly evocative.
Notice the poem begins 'Saw' – there is no time to
write 'I', and this conveys the sense of hurry. Also,
phrases like 'green like moving newleaf sunlight',
capture a sense of vitality and movement. The 'green' of
the final line is literal and **metaphorical** (see Literary
Terms). It is hurrying literally for the green camouflage
which protects it; but equally, the green of its life is the
spring or goodtimes, or essential meaning which it was
born to do.

WAITING FOR THELMA'S LAUGHTER

This is a poem of suspense. Thelma wants to solve the
world's problems the way she does her living room. She
also wants to end injustices of all sorts. She's so
impatient because she has so many dreams that her
head can hardly hold them. Meanwhile her children are
madly running round breaking up her house. The poet

Thelma's laughter watches knowing the moment will come when Thelma
is infectious and will see the funny side of it all – and burst out laughing.
helps others. That kind of laughter is so powerful, it's a tonic for
everyone.

COMMENT The power of the poem is in the contrast – without the
laughter Thelma would go mad or despair. With it her
desire for a better world is admirable.

GLOSSARY lil little

THEMES, LANGUAGE & STYLE

Key themes for Grace Nichols revolve around the roles
and strengths of women, slavery, oppression and
freedom in the context of Black people, children (and
with a particular concern for their hunger) and child-
birth, and sexuality. There is also in her work a preoccupation with the spiritual, but not in a conventional
sense: in fact her 'gods' have female qualities which
links directly back to her central concern with women.

We find that many of these themes are interwoven
together in her poems: 'Waterpot' shows us the
strength and dignity of an oppressed, black woman. So
does 'We the Women', 'Of course when they ask for
poems about the 'Realities' of black women', 'Ala',
'Caribbean Woman Prayer'. These last two poems, of
course, also touch on the supernatural – the goddess
Ala, on the one hand, and the Prayer to the five
personed God on the other. If we contrast the tone of,
say, 'Be a Butterfly', 'Iguana Memory' and 'Those
Women' with these last two, there is a tremendous
difference. These last three poems are full of an
optimistic vitality. In this sense Grace Nichols's poems
could be said to cover a wide range of human
experience and emotion.

Men do not emerge in a particularly flattering light in these poems, except in 'Like a Flame'. However, it is quite interesting that the poet's concern for children is generally unisex: they are children, not male or female. They are loved for what they are, and enough food for them (or its absence) is frequently alluded to, and clearly moves the poet deeply: see 'Of course when they ask for poems about the 'Realities' of black women', 'Caribbean Woman Prayer', 'Be a Butterfly' and 'Praise Song for My Mother'.

The language and style of the poetry is generally direct and straightforward, whether it is written in English or Creole. Traditional forms are largely eschewed in favour of more immediate linguistic effects: repetition of words or lines, echoes of liturgical language from the Bible and prayer, exclamations and commands. **Compound words** (see Literary Terms) are used but not excessively; and their meaning is always clear from the context – they help in fact to give an fillip to the meaning the poet wishes to convey. The poet is unflinching in using words to depict extremes of happiness, 'Like a Flame', or pain, 'Ala'.

A *Identify the poems from which these words are taken.*

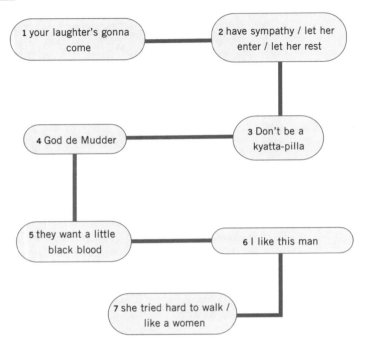

1 your laughter's gonna come

2 have sympathy / let her enter / let her rest

4 God de Mudder

3 Don't be a kyatta-pilla

5 they want a little black blood

6 I like this man

7 she tried hard to walk / like a women

Check your answers on page 96.

B *Consider these issues.*

a How Grace Nichols explores the theme of slavery.

b What Grace Nichols's attitude is to children.

c How Grace Nichols views the role of black women in society.

d How Grace Nichols uses language to achieve effects.

e The use of the supernatural in Grace Nichols's poetry.

FLEUR ADCOCK

BACKGROUND

Fleur Adcock was born in 1934 Papakura, New Zealand, and emigrated to England in 1963. She worked in the UK as a librarian and freelance writer. From an early age Fleur Adcock practised poetry and regards the question of whether women can 'really' be poets as old-fashioned. It is often remarked that her work is 'cool' – her voice distinctive and understated – and that she is not overly influenced by the various poetical trends of writing. Her range of interests is wide, and so her poetry ranges from the autobiographical to impersonal narrative. Her degree (first class honours) was in Classics, and this has led not only to her translation work, but also to a wide appreciation of poetic forms and their use. Technically, she is extremely adroit.

LOVING HITLER

The title is almost a contradiction in terms to the modern mind.

The poet recalls an incident in childhood when she was six years old. A family group during the Second World War sit listening to a propaganda broadcast from the traitor, Lord Haw-Haw. The poet realises that by using Hitler's name, she gets the attention Hitler gets. At school being in love was a necessary requirement for a girl. So why not love Hitler? The six year old compares loving the local lad Albert, who helps with the milking, with loving Hitler. One point in Hitler's favour is that he doesn't mock the girl. An abrupt final line brings her to her senses – Albert may laugh at her but he really was preferable to Hitler.

COMMENT

This poem explores the reaction of a young child to the war. It is interesting because on the one hand the great battle between good and evil doesn't mean much to a six year old if they're not getting enough attention. But on the other hand, the six year old is perceptive about the kind of person Hitler is: famous, yes, but 'you never heard him laugh at people'. The fact of preferring Albert suggests that even a six year old is aware of how unnatural Hitler was in his failure to be able to enjoy the small foibles of human beings.

The language of the poem is very appropriate for a six year old – notice the way fundamental points are repeated by repetition: Haw-Haw (stanza one), Hitler (stanza two), attention (stanza three), Hitler (stanza four), Hitler and Albert (stanza five), and finally Albert in the last line.

GLOSSARY   **mini-proto-neo-Nazi** small-first-new-Nazi

OUTWOOD

The real journey for the young girl is the one of growing up.

Outwood is the school the poet as a young girl goes to in the morning. Her journey is marked by the flowers that she notices and travels through. At school she seems solitary. She writes poems and imaginatively involves someone called Peter – company that she wants. At home she teases her little sister. Bikes are associated with adulthood.

She is looked after by Doris, who takes her for a walk with her soldier friend. The walk again is through the

flowers that the poet notices. These are beautiful and
their names and descriptions – 'beds' and 'smock' –
mirrors a close association with human clothing and
comfort. Doris, however, is not really interested in the
poet – doesn't notice that the girl has damaged her
dress on the vegetation. Doris is much more interested
in being with her soldier, and the poet finally sees the
soldier leaning across Doris – the pink of her blouse
recalling the 'rose-pink with beds of campion' – and
their voices becoming as soft and attractive as the
petals.

COMMENT   The poem shows us a sensitive young girl – living in
her own fantasy world – extremely observant of the
beauties of nature. Really, she would like a friend like
Doris's – Doris has her own 'Peter'. The love talk of the
couple is put in the context of the beauty and
naturalness of the flowers that have already been
observed. But all is not completely idealistic: the plants
also contain briars that create snags, and the journey in
the first **stanza** (see Literary Terms) produced smudges.

EARLSWOOD

The air-raid shelters of school were not very pleasant,
and even the singing in them was as mechanical as
doing arithmetic. By contrast air-raid shelters at home
were much more fun: by day it was a table, by night a
protection. They had great fun setting up what was
effectively their 'camp' – it became a social activity. And
while the raids were going on they could play cards by
torchlight. It was safe and romantic, although their
mother curiously seemed completely stressed by it.
However, once they took in a neighbour who had been
bombed out of her pub, then things became a little
cramped. The woman had her arm injured, but despite
this could dress herself and seemed cheerful enough.
The poet wonders if she imagined things – the woman

At first, taking a neighbour in is fun – but she's wounded.

groaning in pain and broken glass coming out of her hair. Just after the woman arrived, the children were sent away to Leicestershire.

COMMENT   The form of the poem is in triplets (see Literary Terms). Notice the first six stanzas (see Literary Terms) have a near rhyme scheme: the first and third lines have some sound echoes: tunnels / decimals, fun / den, us / -esses / us, head / bed and so on. This creates a jaunty effect appropriate to the fun they are enjoying. Perhaps exact rhyme wouldn't be quite right – the off-rhyme reflects the slightly unreal situation they are in. But even the off-rhyme disappears by the seventh stanza – and this reflects the new level of serious that Mrs Brent brings to the situation.

NATURE TABLE

Various school children study nature. Ben is trying to count the number of tadpoles in an aquarium. Heidi is also looking whilst having a snail on her knuckle. Matthew is drawing a worm – he put one down Elizabeth's neck before. The worms now are locked in their wormery, eating mud. Matthew's eaten mud too. Laura's inhaling the scent of a daffodil. Tom's imitating the shape of a snail's belly squashing his nose against a window, hoping some bird will be fooled by his impersonation. Outside the window the birds ignore him and carry on squabbling over crumbs of food. Ben's now constructing a home made of leaves for the snails. Heidi's worried the tadpoles will eat each other and is trying to talk them out of it. Matthew, on the other hand, hopes they do eat each other. A shaft of sunlight makes Tom's hair seem blonder; makes Laura look up from her daffodil and sneeze; sends the tadpoles wild with movement. Clouds return, all grey and wet looking. The wind picks up, rattles the window, and hail stones now mix with the birdseed.

Fleur Adcock expresses a great delight and curiosity in the natural world.

COMMENT   The poem describes the children as much as nature.
Notice how the hail in the final stanza (see Literary
Terms) indicates the threat that nature poses to its own
life forms. The poem delightfully describes nature and
the children, but is not too idealistic about either nature
or the children.

TADPOLES

Tadpoles are described in all their minuteness and
detail. The poet is fascinated by them as she was by her
own grandson, once a tadpole himself. At that point
the poet wasn't actually a grandmother – but it was
something she had to look forward to.

What's amazing is how the glory of a grandchild
derives from the messy fluids that make up the
reproductive process. Imagining the development of a
child in the womb is like the interest that tadpole
watchers have in their tadpoles.

There is a touch of   The poet has learnt from watching tadpoles – there
sadness in that she   is a link between tadpoles and humans, and all life
cannot be with her   generally. The tadpoles that the poet had grew up
grandson – but   to be frogs, and these may even have been the
frogs, too, tend to   ones that became grandparents to the tadpoles
lead reasonably   she is now watching. Oliver, her grandson, is now –
autonomous   frog-like – bouncing and hopping about, but far away
existences.   from her. She'd like to, but she can't, call him over
                         to share with her the experience of watching the
                         tadpoles.

COMMENT   The poem is a deep appreciation of the beauty and
interconnectedness of nature. Notice how at the end
her own grandson is described in terms of a green
track suit – which is a natural and froggy colour – as
well as being able to hop and bounce: again, frog-like
qualities.

GLOSSARY   **glup** a **neologism** conveying an **onomatopoeic** (see Literary Terms) delight in what the juices represent to her (compare with sounds of *glut, gulp, gush*)

FOR HEIDI WITH BLUE HAIR

Compare Fleur Adcock's view of teachers in this poem with Liz Lochhead's 'The Teachers' and 'The Prize'.

This poem describes a real incident when the god-daughter, Heidi, of the poet went to school with her hair dyed blue. Heidi is sent home on a technicality: there was no school rule against dying the hair, but blue was not a school colour. Heidi at home in the kitchen is in tears, but is supported by her father. He rings the school and makes excuses. Basically, Heidi is a well-behaved girl and this is just a fashion. Heidi finds her father's support comforting. Feels better. Her father finally states to the school that his daughter had his full permission to do it. While he's telling the school this, Heidi chips in with extra arguments for keeping the hair: it cost a lot and won't rinse out. Underlying all these reasons is an unspoken one: that Heidi's mother has died. But the argument against the school was already won: Heidi was a well-behaved girl; the teachers made various noises but finally gave in. When Heidi returned to school the next day her black friend had her hair dyed – only in the school colours. The battle was won.

COMMENT   Heidi has overcome the death of her mother, and her father's support at this vulnerable time was exactly right. We can contrast the 'freedom-loving' father with the teachers who 'twittered' and 'gave in'.

THE TELEPHONE CALL

The mysterious 'they' ask the poet if she is sitting down. They have something big to impart. She learns she's won the top prize in a lottery. They ask what she would do with a million pounds or more. Her **imagery** (see Literary Terms) is particularly descriptive. They advise her to give vent to her feelings. It's then that the poet remembers she hasn't entered a lottery. But her name has been randomly selected. This is amazing – so amazing she admits she'll only be able to believe it when she sees the cheque. Then they tell her: there's no cheque, no money, they deal in experiences. It was a great experience to be told you had won – to imagine you were going to have a million pounds – this was something to remember. They congratulate her and the line goes dead.

The Lottery Company does not make false claims, though its call does prove a cruel hoax.

COMMENT   This is an extremely amusing poem that grows ever more relevant to society and people's desire to win lottery money.

THE CHIFFONIER

The poet's mother has shown her a chiffonier, a small sideboard. The mother is pleased her daughter likes it; but she is uneasy. This particular chiffonier is exactly like one mother used to have. It's light enough to be sent by sea when her mother dies and can contain other gifts. This thoughtfulness is typical of her mother. The poet blesses her mother but the uneasiness returns: mother has a weak heart. She asks how often she can come home and find her mother still alive? The poet argues her mother has twenty years to live; the mother thinks that they'll be no long illness, just a sudden popping off one night.

The poet is amused by the thought of her mother's sneaking off – like a truancy from school. She thinks of her mother, seeing her looking quite ageless, like the poet herself. She finally thanks her mother for the furniture she has found for her, and the fact that it is so linked to her mother's youth. But the truth for the poet is that she only values this because her mother does;

and what she needs to do is tell her mother while she's still alive that she'd much rather have her mother living than her chiffonier.

COMMENT   The poet comments that she thinks of rhyme as a 'component of light verse'. Thus, the choice of rhyming couplets (see Literary Terms) is a way of keeping the tone light whilst exploring the heavy subject matter. Not all the rhymes are end-stopped; the enjambment (see Literary Terms) creates a conversational flow, which is appropriate to the 'dialogue' that the poet is basically having with her mother.

GLOSSARY   Art Nouveau European art style of the early twentieth century

THE KEEPSAKE

A friend of the poet has leant her a book called the 'The Keepsake'. The inscription was particularly apt, as both were librarians: the loan was to be perpetual. The book was an early-nineteenth-century annual which facilitated chaste flirtation between ladies and gentlemen. Many of its pages contained double entendres (see Literary Terms), larger than life romanticisms, and stereotypes of unfulfilled passion.

The word 'intercourse' is a great example of double entendre: meaning primarily 'social communication' in the nineteenth century, but now more strongly connoting sexual union.

A group in the friend's house theatrically explore the book. Five weeks later the poet meditates on the foreboding inscription – just yesterday her friend died while taking a walk. So, she is left with the book – so the perpetual loan becomes a dying bequest. The poet rereads the characters in the book, tries to sleep, but now she can't see the funny side. She just can't stop crying.

COMMENT   The title of the poem is a pun (see Literary Terms): 'The Keepsake' is the title of the book she keeps, but it is also of course a literal keepsake and reminder of her

The poem is
written in eight
regular stanzas;
the rhyming scheme
is abcbac, although
the rhymes are not
all perfect. Use of
inexact rhymes
helps maintain a
conversational air.

dead friend, Pete Laver. The poem is an elegy
(see Literary Terms) and it is useful to compare it with
'The Chiffonier', which while not exactly an elegy
because the poet's mother is still alive, yet nevertheless
uses rhyme for a similar sort of purpose: namely, to
make the dark emotions a little lighter.

Notice the clever separation of the 's' from 'la Comtesse'
– walled up as it were at the beginning of the line – a
nice technical touch.

GLOSSARY   **Gothic** a style which is sensational, barbarous and romantic

THE PRIZE-WINNING POEM

The poem simply outlines what a poet needs to do in
order to win a poetry competition. The tone is light and
having given a number of rules the poet concludes that
there is really only one: to win, a poem has to be good.

COMMENT   The advice in the poem is good, and could provide an
interesting checklist with which to approach any poet's
work. Nowadays, of course, it will not only be typed but
word processed.

The terms used in the poem can be found in Literary
Terms.

STREET SONG

This is a song of menace and violence. Various loca-
tions in Newcastle on Tyne are mentioned in order to
point out that somebody like the Yorkshire Ripper
could be waiting for them there. Just because the
Ripper has been caught does not mean we should
assume that he is not there: there's more than one
Ripper, and the only thing that is certain is that he's a
male.

Comment   This poem again shows the poet using rhyme to deal
           with a dreadful subject matter: serial murderers like the
           Yorkshire Ripper. The purpose of the poem is to act as
           a warning to other women: the final advice, 'Wear flat
           shoes, and be ready to run', highlights how vulnerable
           women are faced with these type of men – men who
           giggle, finger something under their coats, and hide in
           the shadows.

Witness

           Three women sit, dressed in – for them – dark,
           unusual clothes, smoking cigarettes and waiting to be
           called as witnesses for a trial. They peep through to the
           witness box where a woman – a heroine – is
           interrogated. The questioning sounds harsh and the
This poem can be   future of the heroine's child is at stake. Men are
usefully compared   effectively trying to get under women's skirts in
with Liz   order to expose what they find there. What they want
Lochhead's 'An   to find is justifiable blame: women cause violence
Abortion'.   (because they are hysterical). The three witnesses worry
           that they won't gaffe when they have to go to the
           witness box. They imagine the men they can't see in the
           courtroom: the judge and lawyers, all dressed in dark
           clothes. The women prepare themselves, careful not to
           let their cigarettes smudge their clothing. Clothing
           which weakly imitates that of the men within. They
           wait.

Comment   This is a powerful poem which is complementary to
           'Street Song'. 'Street Song' exposed the dangers
           women suffered from men who operated outside the
           law; 'Witnesses' shows an almost worse danger that
           derives from men operating within the law – in fact,
           being custodians of it. Essentially, women are victims
           of the system. In one sense the poet and her two
           fellow witnesses are there to witness on behalf of

Joan of Arc. However, they also witness to the inhumanity of the system by virtue of seeing it in operation. The description of the witnesses as 'witches' (from Shakespeare's *Macbeth* – the Scottish play – that is, outside England, and so England's laws) and the choice of heroine as 'Joan of Arc', who was burnt as a witch by the English, is telling: both derived their power from supernatural (although arguably different) sources, and saw more than was 'natural'. In that sense they are all rebels against the established order – the dark clothes that embody injustice. The poet's contempt for the men involved in these proceedings is vividly expressed in her **imagery** (see Literary Terms) of 'ferretings under her sober / dress, under our skirts and dresses'. Basically, the law would appear to involve an almost voyeuristic violation of women. Yet, for all that anger and contempt, they 'wait to be called' and wear clothes 'unlike ourselves' – there is a fatalistic sense overhanging the proceedings.

LAST SONG

One is reminded by the poem of how pleasing the symmetry of the human body is.

This is an apocalyptic poem depicting the end of the world. The poet bids farewell to what we now know. The two-sided symmetry of mammals, and even of insects, may well disappear. Only creatures living under the sea are asymmetrical. But their plight may well become ours. When this world's gone completely wrong, then oddly shaped creatures will rule.

COMMENT   A warning about what might happen, and given the state of the world this is ever more relevant. However, it is extremely good humoured and amusing, rather than being a shocking or terrifying.

THEMES, LANGUAGE & STYLE

Fleur Adcock's poetry is very much concerned with incidents and stories: war time recollections; children at school and growing as part of the natural process; gifts from a telephone call, from mother, from a dead friend, and from attempting a poetry competition; women in a violent male society, which ultimately predicates an end of the world. Central themes in this are childhood and growing up, family, death and violence, and women as victims in society.

Because her poetry is intimately related to story telling the language and style is familiar and accessible; there is little ostentation and convolutions of syntax or grammar. In fact, if we look at her own prescriptions from her 'The Prize-winning Poem' we find little of poetical **contractions**, **clichés**, large meaningless concepts, **archaisms**, or **inversions** (see Literary Terms). Instead, we find a concentration on an important incident – like Heidi's school experience or the poet's own time at 'Outwood' – where events are described and unfold their own significance. Rhyme is used significantly, as the poet commented on her own work, to create a certain lightness: this can be within a very serious subject, such as her relationship with her ailing mother, or the death of a close friend. Many poems, however, do not rhyme – e.g. 'The Telephone Call' – and one is here is looking at her economy of language which is so effective: to gauge this, ask yourself – how long would the story be if it were written as a prose story?

Fleur Adcock as a poet is technically aware of the many resources in the English language.

ᴛEST YOURSELF (Fleur Adcock)

 Identify the poems from which these words are taken.

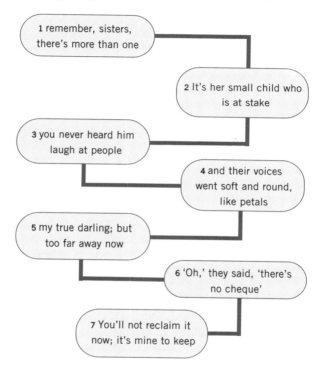

1 remember, sisters, there's more than one

2 It's her small child who is at stake

3 you never heard him laugh at people

4 and their voices went soft and round, like petals

5 my true darling; but too far away now

6 'Oh,' they said, 'there's no cheque'

7 You'll not reclaim it now; it's mine to keep

Check your answers on page 96.

 Consider these issues.

a How Fleur Adcock uses narratives in her poetry.

b Fleur Adcock's views of how women should behave in a male-dominated society.

c Fleur Adcock's relationship with her mother.

d How Fleur Adcock uses rhyme in her poetry to achieve certain effects.

e Fleur Adcock's advice on how to write good poetry.

CAROL RUMENS

BACKGROUND

Carol Rumens was born in London in 1946 and has worked as an advertising copywriter and poetry editor. Her poetry has been greatly influenced by the pioneer American women poets of the 1960s, Sylvia Plath and Anne Sexton. There is a particular political flavour to her work, whether it be considering feminist issues or political issues relevant to specific countries. Underlying this political interest is an acute intelligence and a great compassion. She is realistic about what poetry can achieve compared with, say, the mass media, but sees it as important because it fundamentally touches on an area of importance to her: the exploration of emotional truth.

AT PUBERTY

The poem describes the emotional and physical changes that come over a young girl at puberty. As a result the world seems renewed. A girl becomes more aware. The class are singing a song with the line, 'Come, dear [month of] May'; they feel awkward. May is traditionally love's springtime. The girl herself is experiencing intense feelings for the music teacher who flirts, but is indifferent to the girl.

The language of the poetry very much sees human – or secular – love in religious terms.

The wind becomes a **symbol** (see Literary Terms) for the girl's hunger. Nuns, who control the school, do not want to see what is happening. It is miraculous – how in the midst of the dowdy furniture love's miracle shines. For a whole year the pale girl pines for her indifferent teacher. As abruptly as it began, the feelings for the teacher vanish. Only an enormous gap is left between them. The teacher needed nothing from a child who would have promised her everything.

COMMENT

The ending of this poem is complex. The 'woman who needed nothing' is on one level the music teacher –

hard and self-sufficient. However, the girl matures into a woman, and the feelings vanish – she no longer needs, or loves, the teacher. In that sense the poem is also about the divide between the girl's childhood – which promises so much in her love – and the adulthood when she needs nothing and the promise is gone. The difference, reflected in 'nothing/everything', is a stark contrast.

GLOSSARY   St Bernadette girl who claimed to see the Virgin Mary saying 'Immaculate Conception'

THE ADVANCED SET

The poem explores growing up in the context of the mysteries of adulthood. Three uncles' photographs stare out from the wall. Their faces gave nothing away. Grandmother confirms that they never spoke when they were together in her house, and ate their meals separately. One went to war; one moved to the seaside; the other lived alone in Tonbridge. They were never involved in the poet's life. They did well to die before she grew old enough to mock their pretensions: the truth is, for all their mystery, they were just ordinary people.

COMMENT   The poem explores a common experience: adults seem incredibly mysterious, even wonderful, to young children. And this is enhanced by the snippets of gossip they receive from their own parents – 'tortured', 'mistress', 'port-wine' – all point to a rich life style that the child can scarcely imagine. The tone of the poem, then, is one of relief: they were just ordinary people!

A DREAM OF SOUTH AFRICA

The unfulfilled dream belongs to the poet's father. He'd spent his life at sea, and everything for him had sea connotations. Later, he worked as a clerk. Her father seemed under a cloud. Drink provided a seductive solace – recalled time spent in South Africa. Her father never expressed doubts about his old way of life. Once he talked about retirement in South Africa. This horrified the poet. Later, things went wrong. He missed his opportunities. He loved the names of the big shipping companies, but somehow he went off-course from them. He had a family to support, and so he kept on labouring for them – till he died.

COMMENT

The final line fails to rhyme at all, but the word 'horizon' does echo 'done' and 'down' quite appropriately.

Emotion is kept firmly in control in this poem by the tight **stanzaic** structure – six **iambic pentameter** (see Literary Terms) lines – with a flexible rhyme scheme (abbacc). Flexible here means that words like 'colours' are rhymed with 'climbers'. Also, the pattern shifts in the last three stanzas to (ababcc). The details of the story do not seem 'forced', but emerge naturally. This makes them more convincing, and the attitude of the poet less judgemental: clearly, her father's life is sad, but there is, too, a sense of heroism in his final journey.

OVER THE BRIDGE

Three stanzas describe 'cowboys', or what might be called 'yobs' going about their business in London. They participate in the usual bragging. Some are just ten years old. They exhibit a curious mixture of affluence and deprivation. They love the city and spend their time exploiting it. School cannot hold them in, although they should be there. On Westminster Bridge they gesture obscenely, and move increasingly away from the centre of power. They are lost. Big Ben, the clock, a symbol of history and of power has nothing for them.

COMMENT

This is a vibrant and sad poem. For all their confidence and energy the 'lost boys' situation is desperate:

civilisation as **personified** (see Literary Terms) by the clock's 'proud face' is machine like, and implacable. They have 'disinherited' themselves. Their fate is ultimately beyond the 'gold' and in the darkness of oblivion.

ONE STREET BEYOND

On 'Over the Bridge' the children are responsible for their own fate; in 'One Street Beyond' the children are more victims of the system that will not allow justice or love.

Out at all hours, children whom no-one is able, or wants, to keep track of. These children engage in all sorts of empty activities – the poet lists them. All through the summer holidays the process continues, which hardens these children. They have fathers who leave without a word; and mothers, tired and yelling. But the children create their own broken worlds and never listen to their mothers. Once they began with clean clothes and faces; but they always end up on a street where justice and love can never reach them.

COMMENT

Again, young children are the focus. We are beginning to see the kinds of experiences that mould the kind of teenagers they will be. The poem's tone is more sympathetic: we see what they might have been in the failure of their parents to sustain them. The use of the **present participle** (see Literary Terms) – e.g. skirmish*ing*, slid*ing* – creates two senses: one of on-going action – these problems continue in these ways forever; and of mindlessness – the lack of a main verb in the first sentence enacts the directionless state of the children.

RULES FOR BEGINNERS

The poem depicts aspects of working-class life: aspirations to something better are inevitably betrayed by more immediate concerns. Education comes to mean being an adult, and that means having a good time. This leads to pregnancy. Getting pregnant leads to being a mother, and this is not so enjoyable. Good times become equated with having O Levels – a 'real' education. Such a real education means leaving your own children with someone else, and having affairs – 'night-school' now has a new meaning. What the mother learns is that having 'fun' is best, so best not to have children at all and keep your figure looking good.

COMMENT This is a **sestina** (see Literary Terms) – a complex form in which the word endings of the first six-line **stanza** (see Literary Terms) are repeated in varying patterns in the remaining five six-line stanzas, and all six words are included in the three-line **envoi** (see Literary Terms) which concludes the work. This creates a circularity of effect which is appropriate particularly when the theme *Notice the pun on* or subject matter involves some aspect of repetition. In *O Level and the* this case the circularity with which the young girl *idea of not being* rejects her parents' advice, ends up a mother anyway, *pregnant – i.e. the* and then gives her own advice, which recommends a *stomach remains* certain type of education. Six words are central: mother, *'level'.* Disco, O level, children, nice and adult. The poem is built on the tensions between these.

TWO WOMEN

The poem recounts the life realities of two women: one, the professional, who thinks for her living, and who can manipulate the world. Her hands are clean because she does no manual work. She is very much in control. She returns to her home in which there is a very different sort of life. At home she no longer is of primary importance: she's a manual worker – overworked and angry at her predicament. She never meets the professional woman – they simply can't be brought together.

COMMENT The two women are the same person. Women may well be fully professional people with a standing in the world, but in order to be a 'true wife' they become skivvies or servants at home. These schizophrenic aspects of their being can never be emotionally or logically reconciled. Women themselves do not face the issue: it would torment them if they did.

BALLAD OF THE MORNING AFTER

The title suggests a story based on a hangover. In this situation the hangover results not from drink but from love. A woman in a state of intense despair recounts how she reached that condition. There are millions of people and they all believe in love. Believing in it is like a political creed – one she has abandoned. Yet, the **persona** (see Literary Terms) once believed: not in Christian, but erotic love, where real intimacy existed between a man and woman. Instead, she finds childish games and quick sex. The alternative is to find something else to believe in: 'God or Politics' – but she has nothing with which to build any belief.

A 'loving father' can help a daughter escape the chains of domesticity – it is the lack of fathers who stay in 'One Street Beyond' that leaves children helpless and hopeless.

Other women believe in feminism, domesticity and even men. The persona believes in one man that she desperately wants. But he used her for sex. She was a fool – she married someone and then burned with lust in an extramarital relationship. The burning led to masturbatory fantasy, which simply failed to satisfy. She sees a lost mother and child – her own situation – as symbols for everyone. All in her that is human has been reduced to mechanistic explanations. All that's left is sitting by the window reflecting on the trap she's in. When others describe life, they miss the point: in her condition every bit of it is too much to endure.

COMMENT The poem is in a **ballad** (see Literary Terms) form, which is ideal for narrative. Short lines with the second and fourth rhyming propel the blocks of story forward at a cracking pace. Essentially, this poem tells a story of frustrated and unrequited love.

GLOSSARY   **old work ethic** a Protestant notion that disapproves of pleasure,
            insisting salvation is through hard work

GIFTS AND LOANS

The loans and gifts establish marginal footholds in each others' lives.

Two people at work like to talk together. They find each others' conversation entertaining. There is mutual attraction. A friendship develops. They never quarrel; they suddenly remember each other when at home with their 'routine' partners. There could be a much glossier and satisfying relationship with the friend at work. But it might also give them less.

Here there is a toying with the idea of an extramarital relationship. But these are established and professional people who are – the fading summer evenings suggests – moving towards later life. The passion is not there.

A MARRIAGE

Returning to work on a Monday, the poet is aware that a man she's with is still marked with the essence of his weekend – an essence that's comfortable. The man reveals details of his civilised marriage. She sees the man's wife by a window, smiling as he offers her an apple. It all seems so perfect – golden and cultured. They have led a rich life, following old-fashioned belief systems. She's a Primary school teacher and later will take the garden apples to her 'six-year-olds'. The man goes on telling the **persona** (see Literary Terms) about his wife's achievements: the poet feels she is rather dull in comparison. Then he offers her an apple. This is a critical moment – how does she accept it? She can only do it as a child. To be a woman with him would embarrass her deeply.

COMMENT   The persona's response to the man's happy marriage is ambiguous. On the one hand, it appears to fascinate her

Loving implies equality – how, then, could a modern woman love this man?

– there is something in this picture of nuptial bliss that is appealing and desirable. This may account for the sexual attractiveness of the man. On the other hand, it is perhaps too idealised a portrait – the word 'gilding', perhaps, suggests a golden cover (with the inference of a rotten inside). Either way, the persona cannot be a 'woman' – i.e. a lover – to this man. If the 'Renaissance' picture is accurate, then attempting to seduce him would be shameful – and inappropriate, because his values would expose her own. Equally, if the picture proves unfounded, then the attractiveness of the man is a sham in any case.

GLOSSARY   **burr-like** snagged-on-clothing, seed-like

                 Renaissance literally, rebirth – a period of great learning and culture

UNPLAYED MUSIC

The poet and someone she is attracted to are in a bar. Music is playing, and the whole atmosphere seems involved in the developing relationship between them. Outside the bar the snow reminds them of childhood. A wonderful night – romantic, evocative, drunk! The crowd of people disappear as the two of them engage in their secret life. Back in her dull room, though, she's listening for this person, as she'd listen for a new music. But nothing is played – she only hears the sound of her own heart beating.

COMMENT   A poem that poignantly expresses the joys of falling in love, and the sad despair when it seems unreciprocated. The ending comes as a surprise, given the 'warm' build-up. However, the **imagery** (see Literary Terms), perhaps, gives clues: the **personification** (see Literary Terms) of the green piano, whose heart is 'shut'.

DAYS AND NIGHTS

The poem follows the sequence of events one afternoon, leading to the transition time when nurses change their shifts. Evening then takes over. And finally we see the events of night.

COMMENT   The important phrase is 'very nearly like any other' – there is a similarity between one day, one night and another – and some things don't change – 'the stars keep their distance' – but there is also a slight

The final image   difference. By ranging widely through small local events
suggest both power   to miraculous events of history a sense of continuity as
and importance.   well as change is established.

TIDES

The poet sleeps in a precarious place, trying not to fall in the sea. All its signs seem desperate. She tries to escape, to think clearly. She is far away from meeting her love, and she's 'cool' about it. The sea seems evil. She wants to return south. She finds and pockets a starfish from the beach. At breakfast she attempts to revive it – hopes that it will resurrect itself. But such hope is foolish. All she can do is return home – leave doubt, the village and all its virtues behind. She has to come home – she is in love and there is a change that must happen.

COMMENT   The poem is oblique and difficult. Tides is a **metaphor** (see Literary Terms) that suggests the ebb and flow of feelings and relationships, as well as the more literal fact of the village poised to be destroyed by an incoming tide. Thus, the poet, presumably, has gone north to get away from a relationship that is proving dangerous – but distance does not mean escape. She comments that she is 'Three hundred miles from a pinpoint of a chance / of meeting you' and so the lover is still in her mind.

DECEMBER WALK

The poet visits her father in hospital. She's allowed to take him for a walk in the garden. He's in pitiful state. The poet reflects that the hard trip round the hospital block may well symbolise (see Literary Terms) all life's journey. She kisses him farewell – seeing the day itself as 'the shroud he would be sewn in'.

At his funeral she walks behind him, thinking how light he must now be. She describes the church scene.

The lightness of the This man had been somebody, once. Then he had lost
coffin contrasts his memory. Yet the poet could remember his most
with the weariness typically English and unostentatious quality: never to
of the coffin-bearers hope or believe. He would have approved of even the
and the music. ash his own cremation creates.

A bleak poem, as the title indicates. There are no grounds for hope – yet in that there is a comfort and some strength. Because he believed in nothing, then there is no surprise or disappointment. The imagery (see Literary Terms) of the day – 'breath-white' – is particularly powerful in that day and breath are traditionally positive forces. Here the colour suggests the shroud he will be sewn in.

THE GIRLS IN THE CATHEDRAL

A young girl, Susannah Starr, who died at ten years old, has a small stone dedicated to her memory. Quite why is a mystery; she is not 'famous'. The poet speculates on her history; whoever mourned her death must have been important. Presumably she was buried in the cathedral because her presence with so many hallowed saints would help her journey to heaven, or may be it was because her simplicity and anonymity would contrast with all these 'great' ones. In doing so, she would be evoked – along with our useless pity for her.

COMMENT   Notice the first sentence of the poem: 'Daring to watch'
           is followed by a long list of the great and good before
           the main verb intrudes with 'This small eloquence is'.
           All the others fail to move; Susannah still does, and it is
           her stone which has the verbs of action: 'is … cannot go
           unread'.

CARPET-WEAVERS, MOROCCO

           The poet describes how children weave carpets in
           Morocco. It is a religious experience. They are intently
           involved in it; it furthers the propagation of Islam.
           Eventually, the carpet travels via a merchant to a
           mosque. There it will absorb the prayers said on it.
           These children work hard – experience is their teacher.
           Their fingers create from future visions a view of what
           has happened in the past.

COMMENT   The phrase 'melodious chime' recalls Milton's poem,
           'On the Morning of Christ's Nativity'. Islam is a
           different religion, but the idea of children being
           involved in the work of God is common. As is the idea
           of a music only some can hear – or purpose only some
           can see.

THEMES, LANGUAGE & STYLE

           Carol Rumens's poetry is concerned with people and
           situations, rather than landscapes and nature. She is
           very much an urban poet – the difficulties of living in
           cities and poverty recur ('Over the Bridge' and 'One
           Street Beyond'). Family and class are central
           preoccupations, along with the role of women.
           Relationships between the sexes features strongly, and
           within that how love works or rather, fails to work.
           Death, too, appears in a number of her poems, and

there is, perhaps, with the exception of the 'Carpet-weaver, Morocco', an absence of hope in considering life beyond death. Much of what happens is bleak, and hope in most situations seems illusory. Both Gillian Clarke and Grace Nichols derive strength from their sense of place and belonging; this is absent from Carol Rumens – her strength derives from her own acceptance of the way things are, and from her feelings. The dividing line between this poet's **persona** (see Literary Terms) and her own voice is perhaps not always as clear cut as it might be convenient to believe.

Her style is forceful and direct. She is adept at using both **free verse** (see Literary Terms) and more traditional poetic structures. Her language explores emotional conditions with brutal honesty – she probes and works towards ascertaining motives behind what are, apparently, perfectly acceptable arrangements (e.g. 'Gifts and Loans') between people. She writes in accessible ways – **imagery** (see Literary Terms) is fresh without being overpowering or cluttering – her **personifications** (see Literary Terms) can be especially striking – the syntax is designed to convey, rather than obscure meaning.

Identify the poems from which these words are taken.

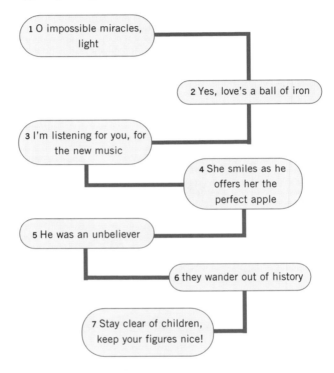

1 O impossible miracles, light

2 Yes, love's a ball of iron

3 I'm listening for you, for the new music

4 She smiles as he offers her the perfect apple

5 He was an unbeliever

6 they wander out of history

7 Stay clear of children, keep your figures nice!

Check your answers on page 96.

Consider these issues.

a How Carol Rumens explores family relationships in her poetry.

b What Carol Rumens thinks of class and urban life.

c Carol Rumens's attitude to love and relationships.

d How Carol Rumens probes people's motives in her poetry.

e The appropriateness of Carol Rumens's poetical forms to achieve her effects.

BACKGROUND

Selima Hill was born in 1945 in London. She left her
education at Cambridge in order to travel. Both her
parents were painters, and despite her vow not to, she
married a painter and has three children. As a child
she felt lonely and writing became her 'friend'. Writing
in this context is a confidante, and we find this reflected
in her style – easy, conversational, intimate. We are
invited in to share. There is not a striving for, or
interest in, the 'bigger' political picture. Instead, there
is a focus on personal experience and its meanings.
Contrasts – be they through photographs, cultures or
mythology – between the past and present in her work
are especially trenchant.

CHICKEN FEATHERS

The poem, in twelve stanzas (see Literary Terms) of
varying length, describes incidents from the poet's
family life, in particular relating to her mother. First,
her mother is viewed in an old photograph. She has a
chicken in her arms – wild-looking. There is an heroic,
god-like quality about her – but the reminder of
Brunhilde also suggests that she will fall by loving some
man. This proves to be the poet's father in the second
stanza. He appears as a curious mixture of
vulnerabilities, but not suitable as the consort of the
'leopard'.

In the third stanza the poet is being collected from
school, and there is a distance between her and her
mother. A contrast between them is highlighted in the
fourth stanza: the poet's hands are warm and clean, the
mother's cold and dirty. The mother shuts up the
chickens.

The father kisses the girl good night, but she wonders
why they think she is asleep. She knows more than

that. She knows her mother is assiduously brushing the
glory of her silver hair, alone in front of a mirror.

Now the poet remembers how her mother enjoyed
chicken. They've gone, but she recalls how they came
running to her mothers' call. In the seventh stanza, her
mother picks flowers for her mother's grave as it is
Easter. Her children can't remember their
grandmother, and don't want to visit a cold grave.

Her father goes to his room and when the poet goes to
call him, she finds him dead. Mother is shocked, but
not grief-stricken. She insists life goes on by making
the poet have her tea.

Later, the poet kisses her mother for what she thinks
might be the first time. Somehow, it was a kind of
illumination.

Her sister says that when father died he was working on
a drawing of a boat poised to disappear. The sister
thought this was **symbolical** (see Literary Terms) of her
father's death. The poet, though, prefers to think of a
boat coming into harbour rather than disappearing out
to sea. She develops the idea: the boat mooring,
someone there to welcome you, and everything full of
life and colour.

In the final stanza her mother has died. The poet reflects on the understanding between them. She visits her mother's grave and sees again that early picture of her in her mind. The question is: was her mother waving to her, or simply brushing away the chicken feathers that drifted in her face?

COMMENT   This is an understated poem. Small details accumulate in significance. The title gives some indication of where our focus should be: the chicken starts off wild-looking, is shut up, is entirely domesticated, and finally its feathers drift like a dream before the mother's face and hair. To state exactly what this might mean is to limit its possibilities, but one interpretation might be: her mother was a god-like woman with enormous potential; she farcically married the wrong man and became domesticated; finally, what she might have been is as substantial as the feathers floating across her still glorious hair.

Tension arises from the perspective of the poet as the daughter. On the one hand, the daughter admires the heroine she sees; but on the other realises that without her mother's domestication then she would never have

Until stanza nine, when a kiss occurs, the mother scarcely seems to care about the poet, and there is no bridge between them.

been. What the poem is then also exploring is the distance that is tragically between the mother and her daughter as a result of these choices.

Equally, the father is a sad figure: solitary and out of his depth with the woman he has dashingly entranced at the ball. The net result is a terrible sense of isolation for the poet. This is not resolved by the end. Her father and mother are dead. But centrally, did her mother love her daughter – was she waving at her, or was she really preoccupied with the feathers of what might have been?

THE RAM

A potent, young male attracts the **persona** (see Literary Terms) of the poem to go to his room. She lies on his bed, watching him undress. The Rams are a baseball team, and he is, **metaphorically** (see Literary Terms), a ram himself. He stands in front of her naked, except for his white socks. He asks her whether she likes it – presumably meaning, his naked body. The expectation is that the star-struck female should ogle and express intense admiration for this quintessence of manhood. But the white socks have sidetracked her: she remembers her grandmother's expression, which is deflationary.

COMMENT   The poem neatly deflates stereotypes. It is well observed in terms of its detail and build-up. The last line is extremely humorous.

DEWPOND AND BLACK DRAINPIPES

A young girl, clearly becoming a handful, is sent away by her mother for an 'Archaeology Week' to study Roman artefacts. Her interest, however, is more in a boy there, though she is rather shy. But one night, whilst working together, he kisses her. Immediately she falls in love with him. Her mother ruefully comments afterwards that her daughter wasn't even interested in the Romans.

COMMENT   The title neatly contrasts the appeal of studying an old and dead culture with living a life in one's own vibrant one. She is proud she is a 'beatnik', one of the first – he doesn't care or understand, but that is immaterial. Awkwardly almost, romance still flowers. It should come as no surprise to the older generation, but it invariably does.

THE FLOWERS

A simple story which outlines the poet's daughter
picking flowers from her grandfather's grave. She rides
her bike with the flowers to the church. The poet
follows behind. Her daughter tends the grave carefully.
The whole job doesn't take her long – about as long as
when she looked after grandfather by making his bed
when he was too ill to do it. Finished, the poet finds it
awkward to leave. But the daughter, without self-
consciousness, knows how: '*It's finished now*'. They ride
home, interweaving their paths on the way.

COMMENT

*'Come' was an
imperative verb
Christ particularly
used (e.g. Matthew
11:28, 14:29,
19:21, 25:31).*

Without being overtly religious, the story functions as a
Christian **parable** (see Literary Terms). The young
child leads the adult – reminiscent of Christ's words
(Mark 10:15). The child sways like 'a candle-bearer' –
thus bringing light into the world. Furthermore, the
child tends the grave, thus acting as a priest. The child,
then, is performing rituals which link her and her
mother to the dead grandfather. '*It's finished now*' recalls
Christ's words on the cross. Flowers living on the grave
hint at life. The **image** (see Literary Terms) of them
riding home indicates how the pathways of the living
also interact – there is a sense of continuity in all this.

DOWN BY THE SALLEY GARDENS

Like 'Chicken Feathers' this poem is based on a
photograph. The poet describes a friend of hers
working in the garden. She is planting. In the background someone is playing the music to the song,
Down by the Salley Gardens by W.B. Yeats. The
woman's back aches from the hard work.

One of her children place her wedding album open on a
table. There is a contrast between their mother now
and how she looked then. The poet describes what she
looked like: raised up (not stooped over, planting),

It would only make matters worse to think about erstwhile beauty.

flowers in her hair (not planting bulbs), and a husband leading her towards the admiration of her lady friends. These same wedding guests and friends are now ghosts who watch her current situation. The music provides an ironic commentary: best if she doesn't listen to it.

C OMMENT

The photograph captures that moment in the past when everything appeared so promising. This is the point of the Yeats's poem – the **persona** (see Literary Terms) of the poem is counselled to take life easy – like grass growing by a weir (a suitably wet and lush environment). However, failure to take advice leads to a fullness of tears. This is what the poet's friend now experiences.

A MONG THE THYME AND DAISIES

The poet, whilst accepting the less than likeable features of age, still finds something wonderful in her situation.

The young poet – as a child – is climbing across a barrow – which seems like a giant – with her family. It seems an enormous journey. When they reach the head of the barrow they make their wishes. They don't think of the future. But now the poet is nearly forty years old. She feels a giant herself – a huge expanse on which children play as she did long before – and nature is growing on her. At the same time, like the barrow (a burial place), she has a wonderful view of the sky.

C OMMENT

The title is significant. Thyme is a **homophone** (see Literary Terms) for time; daisies are associated with death, 'kicking up the daisies'. What, then, seems a quaint trip is also a meditation ('ruminating') on life and death. Of twenty-five lines in the poem, the midpoint is between lines twelve and thirteen – the wishing for the new and wonderful. Again we find this contrast between the promise of the past and the reality of the future. The wishes, which bear no relation to the future, are at the turning point. Notice that the word future has a capital letter: Future; it has become a

proper noun, and as a proper name it has a real address.
It is a place that the child could not imagine, but which
the poet has arrived at.

THE GOOSE

The poem describes a visit home from a young woman,
an only child, who has become a Muslim. Her parents'
home is the Vicarage, suggesting that they are Church
of England and her father a vicar. The last time she was
home was when she drove away to become a Muslim.
Naturally, the parents are extremely excited by the
return. They call the pet goose up from the orchard.
She follows on, hoping for food. In the kitchen the
Cook is preparing the meal – chopping up onions and
crying profusely.

The woman has brought her son to meet his
grandparents. She calls for him and orders him into the
yard. From a window the grandparents watch the child
slit the goose's neck whilst he is calling on God's name,
Allah. The blood runs over his wrists. His voice rings
out loudly. He takes the goose's body into Cook, who is
busy with her preparations.

COMMENT

'She runs up like a lamb' seems an absurd simile for a goose – but the likeness is not in the 'running' but 'being': the lamb is the sacrificial animal of Christianity.

This is a classic case of a poem where the facts speak
for themselves – judgement is difficult. Certainly in
reading the poem, there is a shock when we encounter
the boy – without further ado – slitting the throat of
the animal. Part of the problem with this is the way the
poem deliberately allows us to bask in our familiar
cultural attitudes: the goose is called 'Boo' – we like the
goose – we can easily see it looking for food. Words
like 'Vicarage, orchard, recipe book' create a homely,
friendly sort of atmosphere. We know that animals die
– but not here, not in this way. There is also a
deliberate ambiguity in the fact that Cook is crying –
ostensibly because she's peeling onions. But does this

conceal her feelings towards the 'prodigal' daughter who has returned? We don't know, but by the time we reach Abdullah's dispatch of the goose we are perhaps wondering whether the tears are for Boo (incidentally, the name is perfectly chosen: we say 'Boo' to a ghost – the word evokes shock, surprise, which in fact we – and Boo – are). 'Stuff with sage' is an instruction for cooking the goose – she is reading its funeral rites!

THE BICYCLE RIDE

The poet, light and happy, goes on a bike ride one autumn morning. On passing the church in which her father is buried she comments on its character. She cycles past snatching a glance at her father's grave. This reminds her of the funeral day, and the sandwiches afterwards. These were like pocket-handkerchiefs – ones her father used to help her dry her tears.

COMMENT The feeling of happiness, described as 'like a First Communicant', sets the scene for the final image (see Literary Terms). A communicant is someone celebrating the Last Supper of Christ: they eat the bread, which is His body, broken for their sins.

God the Father will wipe away all tears: Revelations 7:17. Sandwiches, of course, are bread. In the poem they are 'tiny', which is exactly as communicant bread is – the body of the son links the communicant to God, God the father.

DIVING AT MIDNIGHT

A woman diving at midnight with a man thoroughly enjoys the experience. She wants this exhilaration always. Sunbathing, she thinks of those – like the Inuit Eskimo Igjugarjuk – who believe intense suffering and isolation bring someone closer to reality. She then imagines the Eskimo hunting in atrocious conditions. It seems so stark and unprepossessing; but given the conditions, it must be like that.

COMMENT   The poem is in 52 lines of four equal **stanzas** (see Literary Terms). Two stanzas depict the woman's condition – and warm, sunny environment. Two stanzas depict the cold, isolated world of the Eskimo hunter. Both given equal prominence, no judgement is made about their relative worth – only their suitability for those who experience them

BELOW HEKLA

In Hekla the poet is someone; in England she is first an anonymous nobody that the Beatles are not likely to want to hear from.

Some time in the early 1960s the poet works in an orphanage in Iceland. She appears as it were from nowhere, and without associations – yet she is entirely acceptable. She helps with various things. And she's able to have a bath herself in one of the local geysers. She describes herself as a 'short fat English girl', but to twenty-five children she is mother. The leader of the community blesses her for what she does. When she returns home, the children are running to the gate to wish her farewell. They ask her to send love to the 'Beatles' popgroup.

COMMENT   The poem delicately conveys some of the innocence of those days long ago. Notice the language – so many simple direct sentences beginning 'I [verb]'. This is typical of children's language, and so helps create the direct simplicity of style.

THE FOWLERS OF THE MARSHES

The poet describes how three thousand years ago men hunted birds around Thebes in ancient Egypt. They did this with the connivance of the Earth Goddess. In the second **stanza** (see Literary Terms) the poet considers her mother who is like these 'fowlers'. Her world is

haunted by the same gods, and she blithely enters into
it. These gods are not only the Earth Goddess, but also
gods of wisdom and prophecy, secrets and masks.
Meeting her mother she might say something ordinary,
but she's really addressing the God of the Dead. There
is a constant judgement going on with her mother –
what really is in the heart?

COMMENT   The poem takes us back to 'Chicken Feathers'. Clearly,
the poet has ambivalent feelings about her mother, and
the kind of person she perceives her to be. To be a
fowler – cruelly hunting sacred birds (and cowardly,
avoiding any real 'crocodile' challenge) – suggests a
rapacious nature, one made worse by the phrase
'tiptoeing gaily into history' – as if completely unaware
of the damage or hurt caused, as if in fact having a
great party. The 'tiered faience collars' reminds us of the
mother in the mirror combing her 'waist-long silver
hair' – extreme vanity her preponderant vice. 'Hushed'
suggests the lack of communication – the silence of

This poem,   isolation that the child endured. It also connotes a
arguably, answers   condition suitable for hunting purposes – hunting
the question which   whom? At the same time, the word 'oracular' creates
concludes 'Chicken   the effect of someone who is always right and cannot be
Feathers': the   argued with.
mother was not
waving, but   Because it is the poet's mother, it is difficult for the
brushing away the   poet to be judgemental. And the poet endeavours
chicken feathers.   not to be. But the final **image** (see Literary Terms) of
the God Thoth in apposition to mother is surely
revealing. We must remember that her mother's world
is not *like* the fowler's: it is 'the same'. There is a
homophonic pun (see Literary Terms), on fowler:
fouler.

THEMES, LANGUAGE & STYLE

The central theme running through much of Selima
Hill's poetry is family – her relationship with her father
and mother, her experience of growing-up, and the
development of her own daughter as well.
Underpinning this is an unobtrusive religious theme:
big questions are explored in a low key way. For
example, past and present (and by implication, future) –
sometimes highlighted through photographs – is one
such big idea she interrogates through juxtapositioning
various elements.

The style of the language is very simple, down-to-earth,
ordinary even. 'Down by the Salley Gardens' is a critical
example of this, since its title refers to a Yeats's poem
whose tight rhyming, rhythmical and rhetorical
structures are entirely different from Selima Hill's
language. In fact to take rhyme alone, one is not aware
of its presence in this selection of work (there are
occasional occurrences) – it would be too artificial for
her purposes. Rather, she tells a simple story but artfully
chooses significant details and words whose
connotations resonate and link together. She uses
stanzaic (see Literary Terms) structures in order to
pattern and shape her stories. 'Diving at Midnight'
vividly shows this. The poems, largely, seem drawn
from her own personal experiences and memories – and
one feels as if the details must be 'true'. The
relationship between persona (see Literary Terms) and
poet does not seem an issue – the poet speaks in her
voice about what concerns her.

Identify the poems from which these words are taken.

1 This is the Weighing of the Heart

2 Don't listen to the sad music

3 *I love you, Charlie* I said

4 Tonight I kissed my mother

5 I feel like a giantess myself

6 He slits the white neck of the goose

7 My father / used to dry my tears like that

Check your answers on page 96.

 Consider these issues.

a Selima Hill's relationship with her mother.

b The use of significant detail to convey meanings.

c Family relationships.

d How Selima Hill contrasts the past and present.

e The use of personal experience in her poetry.

LIZ LOCHHEAD

BACKGROUND

Liz Lochhead was born in 1947 in Motherwell, Lanarkshire. She spent two years in the USA and Canada, and now lives in Glasgow. Liz Lochhead is also a playwright. This fact suggests what we find in her poetry: an interest in the immediate, the living, the relevant and the 'happening'. Poetry for Liz Lochhead is a way of discovery: the meaning(s) of a poem does not exist before the act of writing, but is uncovered through the process of writing. At school she did not like poetry – it seemed archaic and irrelevant. Her own poetry 'feels' contemporary and deals with important issues that face most people in our society: the role of men and women, injustice, schooling, relationships.

THE OFFERING

The **persona** (see Literary Terms) of the poem reflects on a childhood spent in an intensely religious environment. The first **stanza** (see Literary Terms) expresses the fact that the poet would never return to it. She describes a Sunday in detail: her hand always clutching a coin for the service offering. Details of the service were unpleasant – a sense of awkwardness, unfriendly conformity and ignorance.

The young girl goes to church to give her offering to God, but neither then nor now understands why.

Sundays was also a time for family visitors, which inevitably involved eating ice creams whilst mothers compared their children. By the time evening came there'd be another religious service, this time on the streets. To drown them out other people would turn up the volume of their television sets.

Reviewing the situation, the persona concludes she should never go back to this environment. Foolish to think she could. She would never meet 'their' high expectations. There is no offering she could make.

COMMENT   'The Offering' recalls what happened to the poet as a
          young child. This recollection leads her to realise that
          not only could she not go back, but that she should not
          go back. There is an intense sense of dislike for the
          values that the people in this community represent.
          There seems to be a lack of compassion for others. For
          the child, perhaps, the most frustrating aspect of this is
          that nothing is ever explained, or understood.
          Everything follows a ritualistic pattern: the reasons for
          the patterns are never examined. As a result, no offering
          is given.

THE TEACHERS

          The poem describes her teachers at school. They
          believed ink gave a greater significance to writing than
          pencil. These and other beliefs, along with
          idiosyncrasies of behaviour, are examined. Character is
          revealed. Pupils engaged in various activities, and
          discipline and reward were intimately connected. The
          final line suggests a highly fatalistic world in which
          those who can do things will do them.

COMMENT   This poem is complementary to 'The Offering' and
          takes its theme a stage further. Whereas family and
          community live in traditional ignorance in the former
          poem, in this poem teachers do as well. The teaching,
          such as it is, is traditional. There is an exaggerated
          reverence for ink over pencil – and a list of other
          'received' opinions which bear little relationship to
          knowledge. In fact what emerges is that knowledge is
          fragmentary and irrelevant. Also, that the teachers
          blindly accept tradition and received wisdom.

THE PRIZE

          The kinds of prizes won at the poet's school are
          itemised. 'Perfect Attendance' was a prize, but not one

that meant one had paid any attention to what was
going on in school. Ticks and crosses were valued for
their intensely personal associations. Winning decided
where one sat. One child became the first to die. The
poet won a General Knowledge quiz. The whole class
was engaged in rote learning.

R EVELATION

The poet sees a black bull penned in a dark outhouse
on a farm. He is frighteningly powerful. Outside the
hens go about their business virtually oblivious to his

The 'revelation' existence. But the poet had always been aware of such a
would appear to be dark force, which threatened anarchy to other female
of the monstrosity animals. The poet, seeing the bull, runs away. She
of the male species: passes cruel boys up a lane. She is so shaken she is
its violent, scared she will drop her eggs. Her hand is attempting
destructive energies. to prevent milk spilling.

C OMMENT

This poem is highly symbolic (see Literary Terms).
There is a contrast between the primitive bull and his
rage for 'anarchy', and the well-ordered farm. In one
sense, it is a poem about the chaos which is always
present in civilisation. But it is also about a bull.
The essential contrast is both with hens, female, and
the 'placidity of milk', the produce of cows, again
female. As the girl herself runs from the farm, she
passes 'big boys' in the lane. These boys are noticeable
for their ruthless and wanton destruction of innocent
creatures.

GLOSSARY   hasp metal clasp
                Black Mass – this is a pun (see Literary Terms) – it literally
                means the bull is a black mass. But Black Mass is also a
                reference to the Devil's Supper – an occult ceremony designed
                to defeat God and order

LAUNDRETTE

The poet describes sitting in a launderette with a group of other people. They all put in their clothes and items to wash, and despite having other things to read seem mesmerised by watching their clothing being cleaned. This is because the clothes and materials seem to reflect something about their owners. In effect, watching the clothes go round is like watching oneself.

AN ABORTION

The poem is an eye-witness account of a cow spontaneously aborting its foetus. Initially, the poet is indoors writing. She sees the distress of the animal, but it is its 'emblem-bellow' – its **symbolic** (see Literary Terms) cry – that cause her to go out and investigate. She sees something fundamentally wrong with the animal – the description of the cow's convulsing motions is particularly graphic. The poet calls those responsible. These well-fed men arrive from their Sunday lunches, and dismiss her. But she goes back in the house to peek at what is happening. She sees the men disconnect the abortion from the cow. One laughs at a joke as he does so. They leave the cow, who gets up on her knees.

'Guernica of distress' suggests an atrocity is happening.

The poet reflects that left alone the cow would go on licking the abortion, because she was responsible for it. And she would believe that if she licked long enough, the abortion would live. The cow goes on licking until the men return. The cow goes with the men – but seems almost guilty in doing so.

COMMENT

Compare this poem with Fleur Adcock's 'Witnesses'.

The descriptive language here is particularly powerful – the 'barbed words on my desk top' match the events. Consider the verbs used: lolled, spiked, flecked, drizzled, dropped – short, vivid, immediate. They convey a strong sense of action. The process is deeply disturbing and there is empathy with the cow. The men's callous attitudes are contrasted with the suffering of the female. Finally the **imagery** moves towards a **personification** (see Literary Terms): the men are policemen arresting a criminal who 'goes quietly' with them.

GLOSSARY   **emblem-bellow** a symbolic cry – one which exactly indicates its source of distress
lollop clumsy, misshapen

POPPIES

The family are listening to a Remembrance Day service on the radio. A woman has created a kerfuffle by walking loudly in her high heels. This has broken the silence. Father and mother are outraged by this. The sound of the heel striking the ground is like gunfire. Is two minute's silence too much to ask for? Tradition says not. Why, then, did the woman do what she did? There's no excuse for this disrespect – the soldiers themselves died to keep the silence. The poet offers one possible reason: the woman saw the poppies, wanted to use them as a fashion accessory, and dance.

COMMENT   The power of tradition, particularly military tradition, is strong. It is something the poet questions. Perhaps the

The idea of tradition being a suffocating force that must be resisted comes across forcefully in Liz Lochhead's poetry.

most significant phrase is that of the soldiers who 'fell like flies / trying to keep up the silence'. This seems deliberately ambiguous: on the one hand, they were prepared to suffer death in order to preserve civilisation and our ability to stand in silence to commemorate them; but on the other hand, what they have done is 'keep up the silence' – participated in this culture of secrecy and ignorance.

A GIVEAWAY

This **extended metaphor** (see Literary Terms) charts the progress of a love affair with the writing process itself. As the feelings towards the lover change, so do the words that the poet writes. So, initially, she loved and her words reflected this, but a week later she's not so sure – words have to change. There is an idea that the first thoughts you have, written down as they come, best express one's true feelings. But this isn't so – writing is about rewriting, revising. If stuff's been jettisoned, then the writing's the better for it. Writing can be spoilt by a fidelity to the facts. On the contrary, although telling this might be a 'giveaway', inventing feelings is part of the process. Poets show their skill, not their emotions. Yet despite this, the poet for all her long work finds she can't handle the theme – of love – she finds her writing inadequate on this one particular **stanza** (see Literary Terms): she's abandoned it. The love affair was doomed from the start.

COMMENT   An ingenious poem which neatly explores the themes of love and writing simultaneously. There are an amusing set of **double entendres** (see Literary Terms): e.g. 'scored', 'gone to town on it'.

GLOSSARY   **First Thought's Felicity** notion that the first ideas are the best

THE OTHER WOMAN

When one's suspicions are aroused, it's difficult to ascertain accurate information about the 'other'.

'The other woman' is the term used for a woman who is having an affair with another woman's man. She comes between them. Retaliation can reduce the threat to mere irritation, or it can create a very dangerous enemy. The other woman is a liar. Her intentions are entirely sexual and predatory. Yet, everyone says, she's nothing compared with the injured party. But she can be recognised anywhere.

Finally, the other woman is a reflection of the **persona** (see Literary Terms). Seemingly sweet, but really with a twist – one hand does not know what the other is doing. The other woman is sinister and does not mean her man well.

COMMENT

The left hand is traditionally and etymologically associated with the sinister.

Three **stanzas** (see Literary Terms) introduced by the two lines 'The other woman / lies /'. Each time the meaning of 'lies' changes: the first use of it refers to positioning her self physically between the couple; the second use concerns the intellectual untruths of lying; and the third use is where residing is the dominant sense. It's a Jekyll and Hyde sort of existence: within the woman is this destructive and sinister capacity.

GLOSSARY   **bolster** long pillow

STORYTELLER

The poem describes how a storyteller works: at night time when everything was cleared away. The stories were not useless. People could work while listening to them. Nobody would give ill report of the storyteller – her work appealed to all sorts. Her work was like spinning – she'd create a thread they'd all hang on. In the morning, after the story was over, and as people stirred themselves to work, the stories would dissolve.

But in the minds of children they would sleep like bats, and fly out again when opportunity arose.

COMMENT   This affirms the importance of stories and the way they influence communities, and especially the young.

GLOSSARY   **delft** glazed earthenware

THE FATHER

This poem rewrites the Sleeping Beauty story. The loving Father is responsible for a number of mistakes, including – noticeably as a recurring theme – his failure to inform and explain to his daughter what is happening. The suggestion is that the whole drama is really unnecessary if only he'd done the right things. But she – extremely knowing and with a new love – returns to Daddy. He hears her approach with strong mixed feelings.

COMMENT   This links strongly with other poems in which Liz Lochhead accuses the system – here personified by 'the King' – of keeping people in ignorance. The final **stanza** (see Literary Terms), perhaps, suggest that women, or feminism, has come of age: the old patriarchy that the king represents no longer holds sway.

THE MOTHER

This poem is a companion piece to 'The Father'. Various fairy stories are rewritten with a new 'spin'. Mother is not nice. She wants a child but is always dying young, so that one has to question her real desire. *In this world it* That means the daughter is left with the worst mother *would be foolish to* possible: a wicked step-mother. This kind of woman *trust a mother.* prefers all the other children to the daughter, and would rather she were dead. Don't trust such a woman at all.

COMMENT   Events in fairy stories are extreme, and this version of them questions their underlying motives. When we read fairy stories, we accept the actions as given: Liz Lochhead spotlights some of the critical decisions some of the mothers make.

SPINSTER

A spinster reflects on her life. Perhaps she has been too frantically trying to get a partner. Now the time has come to accept that won't happen; she needs to rebuild her life through various forms of self-development. She has to accept, and think positively. She will work on getting things under control.

COMMENT   A sad poem – the repetition of key words and ideas like 'accept', 'frugal', 'crank' suggests that the life proposed isn't really going to be satisfying – it is not the dream she wants, rather the alternative she must face. The use of rhymes nicely points the humour.

EVERYBODY'S MOTHER

The poet describes the typical causes for complaint about everybody's mother: they did not love their child enough, or they smothered them with love. You were not unique. Mother was ice-cold and rock hard – and she'd pierce your heart. When young, she was artistic; also remotely beautiful and made-up. She'd have sex with some butcher in order to feed you. Mother told stories about herself – acts of war and feats of sensuality. Obviously, mother did not help you feel good about yourself – or your body, especially when your period started. However, she did help you look nice at the carnival. And father wasn't anywhere to be found. So, at least mother was there, even if her presence stopped you seeing anything. Mothers never doing anything right.

'Everybody's Mother' and 'Fat Girl's Confession' are both poems which require us to think about our response to the issue.

COMMENT   The ambivalence of the poet's attitude to 'mother' is
           extremely marked in this poem. Each contrast, as it
           were, annihilates the point made before. The opening
           stanza (see Literary Terms) reflects in its broken and
           incomplete grammar what the final line suggests: the
           whole experience of having a mother is confusing. We
           want to blame mother, but should we?

FAT GIRL'S CONFESSION

           In the persona (see Literary Terms) of a Fat Girl, the
           poet tells her story. The girl falls for a man who says he
           prefers the full-bodied kind of woman. They go for a
           meal – she seems to eat rather a lot. He leaves her, but
           she doesn't cry but eats more food by way of compensa-
           tion. She misses the man, but she finds it hard to give
           up eating – she says she has little self-regard. Still, she
           tries, joins a Health Club and exercises. At the end of
           the day it's all to attract the right kind of dishy man.
           The question mark at the end asks whether all this toil
           and pain is worth it? Is it worth doing it for the man?

COMMENT   This is extremely amusing poem, which light-heartedly
           treats a serious subject: namely, what women have to do
           to be acceptable to men. The use of feminine rhymes
           (see Literary Terms) – e.g. Cheery Veneer / Civil
           engineer – contributes towards the light tone and sense
           of fun: many of the rhymes are unexpected.

THEMES, LANGUAGE & STYLE

           The central themes of Liz Lochhead's poetry are
           family, environment and tradition. The roles of mother
           and father are explored time and again, and there is a
           resolute confrontation with all forms of authority which
           are not open or based on rational principles. One senses

in her work what can only be called an abhorrence of blind conformity. In poems like 'The Teachers' this is particularly heinous as these are the very people entrusted, presumably, to enable young children to develop their powers of thinking. Instead, their methods, opinions and traditions stultify young people.

The exploration of the mother and father relationship and roles leads on to the bigger consideration of feminism. Of all six poets under review in this book, perhaps only Fleur Adcock's 'Witnesses' and 'Street Song' poems are comparable in terms of the savagery of their indictment against men with Liz Lochhead's 'Revelation' and 'An Abortion'. (Grace Nichols's 'I Coming Back' is a savage indictment but this, arguably, is as much a racial as a gender issue.) But equally, Liz Lochhead's indictment against mothers, generally, seems ferocious. (Selima Hill, of course, presents the most severe picture of an actual mother.) There is, then, an even-handedness in her attacks, and the principle reason for attacking would seem to be either a failure to explain or a failure to love.

The net effect of these observations is that Liz Lochhead's poetry is characterised by extremes, and these make for a highly dramatic kind of poetry. This, like Carol Rumens's poetry, is not a poetry of landscape, but of the town environments and situations. Her language draws on a wide range of references – particularly religious and literary (fairy stories). She likes to use and subvert common phrases to create an unexpected meaning. Rhyme features and is used skilfully for both comic and serious purposes.

Identify the poems from which these words are taken.

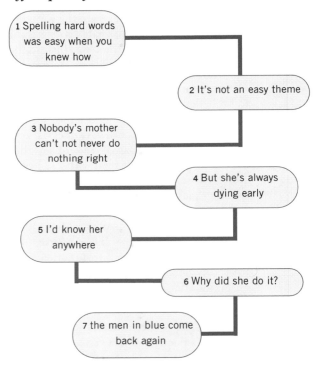

1 Spelling hard words was easy when you knew how

2 It's not an easy theme

3 Nobody's mother can't not never do nothing right

4 But she's always dying early

5 I'd know her anywhere

6 Why did she do it?

7 the men in blue come back again

Check your answers on page 96.

Consider these issues.

a Liz Lochhead's attitude to authority.

b Liz Lochhead's views on motherhood.

c The role of men in her poetry.

d The dramatic qualities of Liz Lochhead's poetry.

e How Liz Lochhead uses folklore in her poetry.

STUDY SKILLS

HOW TO USE QUOTATIONS

One of the secrets of success in writing essays is the way you use quotations. There are five basic principles:

- Put inverted commas at the beginning and end of the quotation
- Write the quotation exactly as it appears in the original
- Do not use a quotation that repeats what you have just written
- Use the quotation so that it fits into your sentence
- Keep the quotation as short as possible

Quotations should be used to develop the line of thought in your essays.

Your comment should not duplicate what is in your quotation. For example:

Selima Hill begins her poem by describing her stepping into the autumn morning: 'I step into the Autumn morning'.

Far more effective is to write:

Selima Hill begins her poem by stepping 'into the Autumn morning'.

Always lay out the lines as they appear in the text. For example:

I step into the Autumn morning
like a First Communicant

or:

I step into the Autumn morning / like a First Communicant

However, the most sophisticated way of using the writer's words is to embed them into your sentence:

Selima Hill begins her poem by stepping 'into the Autumn morning', and then indicates its religious quality by the descriptive phrase 'First Communicant'.

When you use quotations in this way, you are demonstrating the ability to use text as evidence to support your ideas.

Everyone writes differently. Work through the suggestions given here and adapt the advice to suit your own style and interests. This will improve your essay-writing skills and allow your personal voice to emerge.

The following points indicate in ascending order the skills of essay writing:
- Picking out one or two facts about the story and adding the odd detail
- Writing about the text by retelling the story
- Retelling the story and adding a quotation here and there
- Organising an answer which explains what is happening in the text and giving quotations to support what you write

....

- Writing in such a way as to show that you have thought about the intentions of the writer of the text and that you understand the techniques used
- Writing at some length, giving your viewpoint on the text and commenting by picking out details to support your views
- Looking at the text as a work of art, demonstrating clear critical judgement and explaining to the reader of your essay how the enjoyment of the text is assisted by literary devices, linguistic effects and psychological insights; showing how the text relates to the time when it was written

The dotted line above represents the division between lower and higher level grades. Higher-level performance begins when you start to consider your response as a reader of the text. The highest level is reached when you offer an enthusiastic personal response and show how this piece of literature is a product of its time.

Coursework essay

Set aside an hour or so at the start of your work to plan what you have to do.

- List all the points you feel are needed to cover the task. Collect page references of information and quotations that will support what you have to say. A helpful tool is the highlighter pen: this saves painstaking copying and enables you to target precisely what you want to use.

- Focus on what you consider to be the main points of the essay. Try to sum up your argument in a single sentence, which could be the closing sentence of your essay. Depending on the essay title, it could be a statement about a character: 'Heidi is normally a well-behaved young teeenager, but given the pressure she was under her reaction might be said to be typical of that age group'; an opinion about setting: 'Life in East Moors is bleak, but it is nonetheless a close-knit community'; or a judgement on a theme: 'I think one of Grace Nichols's major themes is racism and the way this distorts the lives of both those who suffer and those who oppress'.

- Make a short essay plan. Use the first paragraph to introduce the argument you wish to make. In the following paragraphs develop this argument with details, examples and other possible points of view. Sum up your argument in the last paragraph. Check you have answered the question.

- Write the essay, remembering all the time the central point you are making.

- On completion, go back over what you have written to eliminate careless errors and improve expression. Read it aloud to yourself, or, if you are feeling more confident, to a relative or friend.

If you can, try to type your essay, using a word processor. This will allow you to correct and improve your writing without spoiling its appearance.

Examination essay

The essay written in an examination often carries more marks than the coursework essay even though it is written under considerable time pressure.

In the revision period build up notes on various aspects of the text you are using. Fortunately, in acquiring this set of York Notes on *Six Women Poets*, you have made a prudent beginning! York Notes are set out to give you vital information and help you to construct your personal overview of the text.

Make notes with appropriate quotations about the key issues of the set text. Go into the examination knowing your text and having a clear set of opinions about it.

In most English Literature examinations you can take in copies of your set books. This is an enormous advantage although it may lull you into a false sense of security. Beware! There is simply not enough time in an examination to read the book from scratch.

In the examination

- Read the question paper carefully and remind yourself what you have to do.
- Look at the questions on your set texts to select the one that most interests you and mentally work out the points you wish to stress.
- Remind yourself of the time available and how you are going to use it.
- Briefly map out a short plan in note form that will keep your writing on track and illustrate the key argument you want to make.
- Then set about writing it.
- When you have finished, check through to eliminate errors.

To summarise, these are the keys to success:

- **Know the text**
- **Have a clear understanding of and opinions on the storyline, characters, setting, themes and writer's concerns**
- **Select the right material**
- **Plan and write a clear response, continually bearing the question in mind**

A typical essay question on *Six Women Poets* is followed by a sample essay plan in note form. This does not present the only answer to the question, merely one answer. Do not be afraid to include your own ideas and leave out some of those in the sample. Remember that quotations or close references to the text are essential to prove and illustrate the points you make.

Choose 3 or 4 poems and compare the writers' attitudes to the role of mothers.

Given the number of poems in the book, the scope of the question appears intimidatingly large. It is vital in undertaking a question that one breaks it down into smaller units, and then tackles each unit systematically. First, we need to know which poems we are going to consider. How do we decide this? The best way is to think through what is needed to make a good essay answer. Here are some questions to help that process:

- Which of the six poets deal most thoroughly with the topic? Grace Nichols? Selima Hill? Liz Lochhead? Fleur Adcock?
- Which poets have a consistent view of mothers? Selima Hill? Fleur Adcock?
- Which poets have a range of perspectives on mothers? Grace Nichols? Liz Lochhead?
- Which of their poems provide the most substantial ideas? 'Chicken Feathers', 'The Fowlers of the Marshes', 'The Chiffonier', 'Tadpoles', 'In My Name', 'Ala', 'Caribbean Woman Prayer', 'Everybody's Mother', 'The Mother'
- Which poets have markedly contrasting views on mother? Fleur Adcock ('The Chiffonier' – loves her mother), Liz Lochhead ('The Mother' – mothers are dangerous, not to be trusted), and Selima Hill ('Chicken Feathers' – did mother care for me?)

The above analysis does not purport to be the 'right' answer. Clearly, one might feel that Gillian Clarke's

Letter from a Far Country has more important things to say about motherhood. Whatever you decide, remember that you must be able to manage the information: Gillian Clarke's poem is extremely long and this, if chosen, must be compared with 2 or 3 others. If they are long, too, then the essay threatens to get out of hand.

Part 1

Inform the reader of which 3 or 4 poems you have chosen to compare and why you have chosen them. Selima Hill's 'Chicken Feathers' and 'The Fowlers of the Marshes' because they highly personal views of a real mother. They explore the ambiguity in the relationship. Grace Nichols's 'In My Name' and 'Ala' because these two poems contrast with each other and also present different views of motherhood than Selima Hill's. They are not based necessarily on personal experience but recall the experience of the Caribbean slaves.

Part 2

Explore in depth the first two poems by Selima Hill. 'Chicken Feathers' is the more substantial poem of the two. Dwell on its ideas – how the relationship between the mother and the poet changes over a lifetime; how small incidents are extremely expressive; how the final stanza leaves us with an ambiguity concerning the love of a mother for her daughter. Cite a line that shows for you how strained the relationship is: e.g. 'Tonight I kissed my mother, / for the first time that I can remember'. Sum up the overall impression that the poem creates of the role of the mother. Move on to 'The Fowlers of the Marshes'. How true is your impression from 'Chicken Feathers' in this poem? Is the antagonism more explicit? Is the last line still ambiguous? How are the myths of ancient Egypt used to help understand the present? What line captures the essence of the poet's attitude to her mother? Summarise what you think Selima Hill's attitude to the role of mothers is from your consideration of these two poems. For example, one might describe her attitude as perplexed – she is unsure of what her mother's role is, or how she should respond to it.

Part 3
Now repeat the process for Grace Nichols's 'In My Name' and 'Ala'. Notice here the unambiguous love for a child in 'In My Name'. There is a great deal of tenderness, and the poem is about that most intimate of moments: the moment a mother gives birth to her child and the bonding starts. Pick out a line or two which shows the tenderness. Remember, this will be useful to compare with Selima Hill's experience in the final paragraph. More than tenderness, notice the sacrificial language with which the poem moves to its conclusion: 'For with my blood'. This can now be compared with 'Ala'. Here is a knotty problem: on the one hand the mother is a murderer – she kills her child and so pays for this with her blood. But the tone of the poem is sympathetic. This mother killed her child in order to save it from a life of slavery. Was this love? Or was it despair? What evidence can you produce to back up your opinions? Summarise what you think Grace Nichols's attitude to the role of mothers is from your consideration of these two poems. For example, one might describe the overwhelming impression of the poet's attitude as being one of unflinching love in the face of any adversity. Even the situation in 'Ala', it could be argued, shows a mother who does give her blood for her children – mothers are pivotal in the life of their children.

Part 4
You have looked at four poems in detail and brought out your ideas on each of them, already having begun the process of comparison by linking poems written by the same poet. In the concluding section of your essay you should bring a comparison of all four poems into play. This is not a question of stating

which is best but of comparing them for similarities and differences. Similarities might include the ambiguity of our reaction to the mother in 'Ala' and the ambiguity that Selima Hill experiences in facing her mother. Equally, 'Ala' and 'The Fowlers of the Marshes' both use mythologies to explore the relationships – Ala is a goddess of the dead, as Thoth is also a god of the dead. Differences might include the lack of tenderness that we find in Selima Hill's mother compared with the emotional strength that the mother projects for the child in 'In My Name'. Here we might notice, too, how Selima Hill's poem is written from the viewpoint of the child observing the mother, whereas 'In My Name' is written from the viewpoint of the mother viewing the child that has just been born. We might comment on how effective these perspectives are.

Conclusion   Finally, in comparing the poems sum up what you have learnt. It is good to give a personal comment on your analysis. It may be that your favourite poem is 'In My Name' because you admire the strength, love and determination of the mother. This may be how you think mothers should be. You may also like the realistic way in which the birth is described. Alternatively, you may find that 'Chicken Feathers' is particularly good because you like the way that Selima Hill uses her own life to describe her relationship with her mother. This may make her account seem especially truthful. You may feel that you 'relate' to her situation because you are not sure how you feel about your mother. Using personal response is a valid way of drawing together the threads of an essay – always making sure you stick to answering the question as you do so.

FURTHER QUESTIONS

Make a plan as shown above and attempt these questions.

1 Choose three poems from any *one* poet that particularly interested you. Comment on the ideas and attitudes in the poem, the uses of language that emphasise the poet's points, and why you have chosen these three poems.

2 Choose three poems involving different characters and consider the ways in which they are described.

3 Poets choose very different forms and kinds of language in which to express their ideas. Contrast the work of two poets who seem to you to be very different in style.

4 People have different ideas about what is beautiful and what is important. Which poems made you think 'I agree with that', or 'No, that's not for me'. Compare your reactions to at least three poems in this group.

5 Many of Gillian Clarke's poems describe changes that have occurred in people's lives. With reference to at least two of her poems, comment on some of the changes she is describing.

6 What contrasting ideas can you find in Grace Nichols's poetry? Refer to 'In My Name' and 'Ala', or to 'We the Women' and 'Those Women'.

7 Discuss Fleur Adcock's attitude to men with reference to at least three of her poems.

8 What does Carol Rumens show about her relationship with her father in 'A Dream of South Africa' and 'December Walk'? How does she present the relationship?

9 With reference to at least two poems by Selima Hill, describe her relationship with either her mother *or* her father.

10 Liz Lochhead's poetry often challenges conventional ideas and opinions. Choose two of her poems and show how she does this.

CULTURAL CONNECTIONS

BROADER PERSPECTIVES

The grouping together of Six Women Poets serves a useful introduction to women's poetry in what Carol Rumens anthology refers to as the Post-Feminist period (*Making for the Open; The Chatto Book of Post-Feminist Poetry, 1964–1984*, ed. Carol Rumens, Chatto and Windus, 1985). This is not to suggest that feminism has been and gone, but that its principal battles have been won. There was a time when being both a woman and a poet was generally considered to be incompatible. Feminism, in poetry, as in other areas of life, has challenged that notion consistently over the last thirty years or so. Women now are able to write poetry and command the same sort of respect and interest that was traditionally reserved for (male) poets.

That said, it might be argued that why, then, do we need collections of Six Women Poets? Why not just poets? The answer is twofold. First, there is still generally recognised to be a distinctively female voice. Second, there is still a tendency among influential critics to disparage women poets. The most noticeable example of this is in the use of the word 'domestic'.

Thus, putting together a collection of Six Women Poets serves a double cultural function: it enables readers to see the range and depth of women's poetry; and it reasserts its importance. It would be interesting to ask the question why the poets are ordered in the way they are: in neither alphabetical nor chronological order. It is, arguably, because *Letter from a Far Country*, the first poem in the collection, most powerfully and most directly answers the charge of domesticity by engaging in it head-on and showing its significance in the pattern of our lives. This poem represents in many ways the cultural shift of values that has been occurring in our society over the last thirty years or so.

LITERARY TERMS

allusion/allusive a passing reference to another work

archaisms old-fashioned words no longer in use

ballad song form of poetry, usually rhyming abcb, and with alternately four and three stresses

blank verse unrhymed lines with five stresses (iambic)

cliché a boring phrase made tedious by frequent repetition

colloquial everyday language

compound word words connected to form new meanings

contractions shortenings of words by removing letters and replacing them with an apostrophe

couplet a stanza of two rhymed lines

double entendre two meanings, one of a usually sexual nature

elegy poem marking a death

emotive affecting the feelings

end-stopped rhyme a rhyme which completes the syntactic unit of meaning

enjambment the running on to the next line to find the complete sense of the former

envoi a final, shorter stanza

epistolary in letter form

extended metaphor a comparison which is consistently developed

feminine rhyme usually rhyme of two syllables

free verse *vers libre* – no regular metre, line length or pattern

homily a short moral story

homophone two words spelt differently but pronounced the same

iambic pentameter a line of ten syllables and five stresses, each second syllable being stressed

image a word picture

inversion a departure from normal word order

metaphor unstated comparison

neologism a newly created word

onomatopoeic when the sound of words echoes their meaning

parable short moral tale

pathetic fallacy ascribing human feelings to inanimate objects or phenomenon

persona voice of the poet which is not to be confused with the poet's own opinion

personification a metaphor which compares something to human qualities

preposition part of speech showing relative position of nouns

present participle adjective derived from a verb

pun a word or phrase used in at least two different senses

quatrain a four line stanza

sestina a rare and elaborate verse form comprising six stanzas and a three line envoi

stanza several lines of verse that form a unit

symbolic something representing something else by association

triplet a stanza of three lines. Triplets often imply rhyme

TEST ANSWERS

TEST YOURSELF (Gillian Clarke)

1 Miracle on St David's Day
2 Letter from a Far Country
3 Login
4 Marged
5 Letter from a Far Country
6 White Roses
7 Last Rites

TEST YOURSELF (Grace Nichols)

1 Waiting for Thelma's Laughter
2 Ala
3 Be a Butterfly
4 Caribbean Woman Prayer
5 Of course when they ask for poems about the 'Realities' of black women
6 Like a Flame
7 Waterpot

TEST YOURSELF (Fleur Adcock)

1 Street Song
2 Witnesses
3 Loving Hitler
4 Outwood
5 Tadpoles
6 The Telephone Call
7 The Keepsake

TEST YOURSELF (Carol Rumens)

1 At Puberty
2 Ballad of the Morning After
3 Unplayed Music
4 A Marriage
5 December Walk
6 Over the Bridge
7 Rules for Beginners

TEST YOURSELF (Selima Hill)

1 The Fowlers of the Marshes
2 Down by the Salley Gardens
3 Dewpond and Black Drainpipes
4 Chicken Feathers
5 Among the Thyme and Daisies
6 The Goose
7 The Bicycle Ride

TEST YOURSELF (Liz Lochhead)

1 The Teachers
2 A Giveaway
3 Everybody's Mother
4 The Mother
5 The Other Woman
6 Poppies
7 An Abortion